Longman Handbooks for Lar
General Editor: Donn Byrne

Role Play in Language Learning

Carol Livingstone

BRITISH SCHOOLS s.r.l.
Via Castagnevizza 4 FIUMICINO 00054 ROMA
FILIALE RM - BRITISH SCHOOL
Via Lucullo, 14 - C.F. 00426650586

Longman

Longman Group Limited
Longman House, Burnt Mill, Harlow,
Essex CM20 2JE, England
and Associated Companies throughout the world.

First published 1983

ISBN 0 582 74611 6

Printed in Singapore by
The Print House (Pte) Ltd.

Longman Handbooks for Language Teachers
General Editor: Donn Byrne

The Teaching of Pronunciation – Brita Haycraft
The Language Laboratory and Language Learning – Julian Dakin
Writing English Language Tests – J B Heaton
Visual Materials for the Language Teacher – Andrew Wright
Teaching Oral English – Donn Byrne
Selections from 'Modern English Teacher' – edited by Helen Moorwood
Second selections from 'Modern English Teacher' – edited by Susan Holden
An Introduction to English Language Teaching – John Haycraft
Teaching Writing Skills – Donn Byrne
Drama in Language Teaching – Susan Holden
Communication in the Classroom – edited by Keith Johnson and
    Keith Morrow
Teaching English through English – Jane Willis
Role Play in Language Learning – Carol Livingstone
The Practice of English Language Teaching – Jeremy Harmer

To Molly

Preface

The past few years have seen a marked increase in the number of language teaching textbooks and materials which include role play. Some of these are devoted purely to a number of detailed role plays, but role play is also found as a component of general, integrated skills courses. This is hardly surprising when the current methodological trend, at least as regards the development of oral/aural skills, is towards materials based on language function, and aiming at communicative competence.

Unfortunately, such materials, and their accompanying teacher's guides seldom give *detailed* guidance on how to prepare for and organise role playing in the classroom, and how to integrate this activity into the total language learning programme. Neither is the importance of role playing in a course aiming at communicative competence discussed.

It is these points which this book aims to clarify. In the past seven years I have given a number of teacher-training courses, seminars and lectures on role play, and have accumulated not only course and lecture notes, but also comments, criticisms and questions from the teachers participating. These, together with my own experiences of using role play in the language learning classroom, form the basis on which this book has been written.

I am only too aware that there are a number of problems left to be solved. These deal with the teaching and learning of para- and extra-linguistic features, and the question of the acceptability and appropriateness of utterances in any given context and situation. Before some definitive research results are available on these aspects of language, it will be difficult to incorporate them systematically and effectively into our teaching programmes. Until then, teachers will have to use what knowledge is available, and trust to their own knowledge of, and instinct for, the language they are teaching.

The word 'English' has been used in its broadest sense. The reader should assume it to mean the kind of English he or she teaches, be it American English, Australian English, or whatever. Teachers and students have been referred to as 'he' throughout the book, this being the most commonly accepted pronoun until a word is devised which will cover 'he and she'.

I would like to thank all the teachers and students who attended my courses, and commented on and criticised my ideas and role plays. I am also indebted to Karen and Marielise, who read and re-read the various draft manuscripts and gave me constructive criticism and encouragement, and to Niels, who unravelled some of the knots.

ACKNOWLEDGEMENTS
We are grateful to the following for
permission to reproduce copyright
photographs:

Camera Press Ltd for page 41 (left);
Keystone Press Agency Ltd for page 42;
Longman Photograph Library for page 69;
Syndication International Ltd for page 41
(right).

Illustrations by Michael Davidson

Contents

1 What is role play?

1.1 Role play and simulation

In this book the term 'role play' is used to cover activities where the term 'simulation' might arguably be employed. Textbooks and teacher's handbooks do not always agree on the precise definition of these terms, and indeed some activities may simultaneously involve both role play and simulation. Without wishing to embark on a lengthy discussion of the differences between the two (it can surely be argued that we are all constantly role playing, no matter in which situation we find ourselves), I would like to make clear what I feel to be the main distinction.

Let us assume a class of business people, learning English for professional purposes. They are given a problem to solve at a meeting. The problem and the type of meeting closely resemble those they experience in their daily work, or will experience in the foreign language situation. Each student is given a role which is within his own area of operations (e.g. an accountant is given a role which requires experience and knowledge of figures and finance, etc.). Each student is then asked to work out his own attitude to the problem, and his own strategy for dealing with it. He presents this view at the actual meeting. This is an example of *simulation*.[1]

The same situation, the business meeting described above, can be used to illustrate role play. This time, each student is given particular information about his role, which he must take into consideration. He may, for example, be given the following role card:

> You are Mr Jones, the chief accountant. You want
> the contract to go to Kidd and Co. because you
> know the managing director socially, and he has
> promised to give your son a good job. Try to
> persuade the meeting to accept Kidd's offer without
> revealing why.

1 Simulations need not stick so closely to real life. They may, for example, involve being shipwrecked on a desert island (see K Jones *Shipwrecked!* from *Nine Graded Simulations for Communicative Skills* (ILEA 1974)). The essential point is that the student brings his own personality, experience and opinions to the task.

1

Here the student is not free to present his own opinion, or personal view of the problem; he has to present that of Mr Jones. This is an example of *role playing* within the context of a *simulation*.

On a lower level we might take a shopping example, where a student is given this role card:

> You bought a sweater two days ago. You have
> discovered a hole in it. Take it back to shop and
> explain the problem. You do not want another
> sweater, you want your money back. Be polite at all
> times.

Although the student is free to choose the language he will use to do this, his attitude, the way the situation develops, and its eventual outcome have been decided for him. This, again, is *role play*.

From the language teaching point of view there is little difference between embarking on a role play, a simulation, or a simulation involving role play. All three require careful planning, careful preparation and careful organisation. This is the work that the following chapters set out to explain.

1.2 Aspects of role behaviour

In the unnatural situation of the classroom the students can only simulate or play roles. In daily life outside the classroom we all fulfil in reality, in our own language, any number of roles. At home: the role of husband or wife, father or mother, daughter or son; visiting a shop: the role of customer; visiting the doctor: the role of patient, and so on.

In each of these roles we act differently. We may come home from work, hug our husband or wife, and say: 'Hello darling'. We are not likely to do the same to the doctor on a professional visit to the surgery.

There is a certain range of behaviour which is acceptable and appropriate to each role, and only rarely, and in exceptional circumstances, do we deviate from it.

This set pattern of behaviour is part of our upbringing, our cultural background. The smooth day-to-day functioning of our interaction with others depends on reasonably strict adherence to its unwritten laws. The linguistic aspect is, as far as English is concerned, perhaps the most important part of our role behaviour.

In another language, role behaviour may be very different from one's mother tongue, but the aspects involved are the same.

1.2.1 Formality

We may greet a colleague with: 'Hi there, Tubby', but we address our boss, no matter how corpulent, with: 'Good morning, Mr Smith'. Asking the way of a complete stranger we might say: 'Excuse me, could you tell me where the town hall is?', and on receiving an answer, reply: 'Thank you very much'. If, however, we are looking at a map with a friend, we might say: 'Where's the town hall, then?', and on receiving an answer, reply: 'I see'.

We use more or less formal speech depending on our relationship to the person we are speaking to.

1.2.2 Register

Some of the roles we have to fulfil require the use of specific features of language, i.e. a special register. Occupational register provides the clearest example: two chemists, talking about their work to each other will use many words and phrases from the field of chemistry which makes their conversation difficult, if not impossible for a listener with no knowledge of chemistry to understand. But it is not only lexis, it may also be the whole way of formulating an utterance. A wedding ceremony would not sound quite the same if the officiating clergyman said: 'OK, Bill, so you want to marry Jean here', instead of using the accepted religious register: 'Do you Bill Jones, take this woman . . .?'. On a more mundane level we may tell a friend: 'I've got a rotten pain in the guts', but in the role of patient we would tell the doctor: 'I've had a bad stomachache for two days'. However the doctor, using a more precise medical register, might refer to your: 'abdominal pains'.

1.2.3 Function

Language will also be affected by the use we wish to put it to. Do we wish to express an opinion, to agree or disagree, to persuade or complain? These are all examples of language functions. In any one role we will need a variety of different functions. When meeting a friend we may first need the function of greeting: 'Hello, Joan, nice to see you'; then of enquiring about health: 'How are you today?'; then, perhaps, of inviting: 'How about going to the cinema?', and so on. Similarly, in our role of customer in a shop, we may be merely buying things: 'I'd like a pound of butter', or we may wish to complain about goods already bought; not: 'I'd like to complain', but: 'I'm afraid I have a complaint to make'.

Function, then, is an important aspect to be considered when selecting which language to use.

1.2.4 Attitude

How we feel towards the situation, and towards the other people involved in it, is also important. 'I'm afraid I have a complaint to make' is polite, and shows a neutral attitude. We will choose different language if this is the fourth time we have complained about the same goods, and feel both angry and frustrated: 'This is too much!'.

Just as we must make clear what our own feelings (anger, delight, surprise, etc.) are, so we must be able to recognise these feelings in our interlocutors, and to adjust our own reactions accordingly.

1.2.5 Para-linguistic features

In all the examples given above, the language must not only be selected correctly, it must be *said* correctly.

The angry complaint: 'This is too much!' will have little effect on, and may even confuse the shop assistant, if it is said in a polite, friendly manner. Stress, intonation, rhythm, tone of voice, speed of delivery, pitch and loudness all have to be correct if the listener is to realise that there is an angry and frustrated customer to deal with.

1.2.6 Extra-linguistic features

So far we have discussed only verbal and vocal behaviour. All the examples above could easily be understood on the telephone if said correctly.

Much of the student's experience of the language will, however, be in face-to-face interaction, so it is important to know the appropriate gestures and facial expressions which accompany the language.

The strong complaint above is weakened, and even made confusing, if accompanied by a warm smile. It is made much stronger if the goods are slammed down on the counter.

There are many cultural differences here. Scandinavians, for example, shake hands on many more occasions than the British. Minor embarrassments are often caused by offering a hand which is ignored, or regarded strangely for a few seconds before being taken in puzzled silence.

1.2.7 Acceptability and appropriateness

All the features mentioned in 1.2.1 to 1.2.6 above are interlinking parts of the total 'role behaviour'. If we understand them, and can produce them correctly, the result will be acceptable and appropriate language and behaviour. The following example will serve as a summing-up.

A and B are business acquaintances and as such are normally polite, friendly, but formal towards each other.

A: I wonder if you'd like to come to dinner on Friday?
B: (a) Not bloody likely.
    (b) Yes, I would.
    (c) I'd love to.
    (d) I'd love to but + excuse.
    (e) Delightfully.
    (f) Fine.

We can examine these six replies for acceptability and appropriateness:

(a) is inappropriate to the situation, probably totally unacceptable to A, and does not show the polite, friendly attitude required.

(b) is grammatically correct, but not formal enough. It is therefore not an appropriate response to the question. It might, however, be marginally acceptable from a non-native speaker if the intonation, etc. were friendly enough.

(c) is, on paper, the most acceptable and appropriate. It could, however be said in such a way as to make B sound rude or disinterested.

(d) is subject to the same comment as (c) above (assuming of course, that the excuse is also acceptably and appropriately formulated and said).

(e) is not 'correct' English, but might be acceptable from a non-native speaker if it sounded friendly and 'delighted' enough.

(f) is not formal enough, and therefore not appropriate, but might be marginally acceptable from a non-native speaker.

It has been suggested that native speakers of a language are more tolerant of formal, grammatical errors from a non-native speaker than they are of errors made in points 1.2.1 to 1.2.6 above. This may be because these features are taken so much for granted, and have not yet been examined in any detail, from the point of view of either first- or second-language learning. It is in these areas, therefore, that the non-native speaker may be misunderstood or misjudged without knowing why, if he knows his utterance to be correct on a formal grammatical level.

1.2.8 The immediacy of oral interaction

Many activities take place in oral interaction:

(a) The speaker/listener must understand the situation.

(b) He must understand, and *show* his comprehension of what is being said. This may be done verbally (encouraging 'mmms', questioning 'eh?s' etc.) or non-verbally (smiles, nods, frowns etc.).

(c) He must, if he wishes to speak, listen and look for cues from the other speakers so that he can begin his utterance at an acceptable place. Someone giving up the turn to speak may signal this by 'fading out' his utterance on a falling intonation, somebody wishing badly to speak next may signal this by an audible indrawn breath and lifted hand.

(d) Having initiated his utterance he must select and produce acceptable and appropriate language.

(e) While making his utterance he must carefully monitor the behaviour of the other participants. If this behaviour shows incomplete comprehension of his utterance he may have to rephrase, expand, or completely reformulate it.

(f) He must give signals as to whether he wishes to continue speaking, or is ready to give up his 'turn' soon, so that the other participants may adjust their reactions accordingly.

As many of these activities take place simultaneously, it is not enough merely to be able to select and produce acceptable and appropriate language. The teacher must also make sure that the student is capable of doing so effectively in an activity which at least *resembles* a real speech situation.

1.3 Role play

Role play is therefore a classroom activity which gives the student the opportunity to practise the language, the aspects of role behaviour, and the actual roles he may need outside the classroom. Most students will not need to fulfil in the foreign language the wide range of roles they fulfil in their mother tongue, unless, of course, they intend to live and work in the foreign language environment for an extended period of time. But just as we can never accurately predict what the learners will hear and need to interpret in the foreign language, so we can never accurately predict what they will want or need to use their knowledge of the language for; what situation they may find themselves in, or which roles they will have to fulfil.

We must therefore help our students to a broad awareness and understanding of role-behaviour, and give them extensive practice in using this knowledge.

1.3.1 Roles and the classroom

The type of activity indicated above cannot be achieved in a totally teacher-dominated classroom. Here there are only two roles; those of teacher and student. As with all other roles, these have a set pattern of linguistic and non-linguistic behaviour.

1.3.1.1 The traditional teacher's role

The teacher is the person in control. He makes decisions regarding the materials to be used, the language to be practised, and the classroom activities in which it will be practised. He will probably make only correctly formulated utterances in the foreign language, and these will be clearly enunciated and delivered at less than normal speed of speech. By reason of his authoritarian role he can issue such commands as: 'Sit down', 'Be quiet', (formulations which would be far from acceptable in anything other than very informal social interaction).

1.3.1.2 The traditional student's role

The student should obey the teacher, engage without comment in the activities he suggests, and produce the language he requires. Teachers often require that the students' utterances are preceded by a raised hand, and a clear indication from the teacher that the student may now speak, (a piece of interaction very rarely encountered anywhere but in the classroom).

1.3.1.3 Role play and traditional classroom roles

In order for role plays to be fully effective, the traditional roles discussed above must be forgotten, at the very least for the period of time during which the role play takes place. The student must be free to play his role as he sees it, to speak when he judges it necessary or appropriate: in short, to be his own master.

It follows, therefore, that there is no place in a role play for teacher direction, interference, or even guidance. It is true that the teacher has probably selected the material and directed the language practice for the pre-role play activities, but once the role play has started, teacher direction must stop.

1.4   Activities often confused with role play

Before examining role play in detail, it is relevant to look at some class-room activities which might be confused with role play, but are, in fact, very different.

1.4.1   Play-acting

Students, especially younger learners, enjoy acting out sketches or short plays for their peers or parents. Whether these have been selected from a book, or written by the students themselves, this activity is not role play as the language is pre-determined and learned by heart. This means that the students need not monitor the speech of others with a view to formulating their own contribution to the discussion. No mental process other than memorisation is involved. It does not, therefore, resemble a real speech situation.

1.4.2   Group work

Role play is, of course, one form of group work, but what is being discussed here is the kind of activity where the students, in pairs or larger groups, have a formal language exercise to discuss and complete, some questions to answer, a topic to discuss, or some similar task to perform. In most cases they will have to select and formulate language appropriate to the task and to monitor each other's speech. They will have the opportunity, at least at the advanced levels, of expressing their own opinions and feelings, but they are not playing roles within a situation which resembles real life.

There is normally only one role involved, that of the student playing him-self as student. The main aim of such exercises is that the group completes the task given as linguistically correctly as possible, so such aspects of role behaviour as formality and attitude will only become relevant in so far as they are concerned in the aim of the exercise, not as an integral and neces-sary part of the interaction within the group.

Also, although the groups may be working without the direct participa-tion of the teacher, the teacher can, at any time he or the group judges rel-evant, break into the group work in his role as teacher, and give advice, make corrections, even redirect the course of the group's work. This is not done in role play.

1.4.3   Dialogue work

There are a number of teaching techniques that come under this heading: they will be only briefly mentioned at this point. The word 'dialogue' is used here to mean the type of conversational exchange to be found in most language teaching textbooks. They may also be composed by the teacher or the students. They usually illustrate a structure, some vocabulary, or a language function. They can be used as they are, as in 1.4.3.1 below, or as the basis for further work as in 1.4.3.2 to 1.4.3.4 below.

1.4.3.1   Reading dialogues 'with meaning'
The dialogue, using the teacher or a tape as model, is first used for choral and individual repetition. The aim is to get the students saying the dialogue with the closest approximation to native speaker pronunciation, stress, intonation, rhythm, etc. as is possible at any given level. The students then read the dialogue either in class or in groups, perhaps with appropriate gestures, actions and props.
This is a form of play-acting, which has already been discussed.

1.4.3.2   Class composition
From suggestions given by the students, the teacher writes a dialogue on the blackboard or overhead projector. The dialogue can then be practised as in 1.4.3.1 above.
In this activity the students have to select appropriate and acceptable language to fit the situation, roles, attitudes, etc. These are still, however, only teacher and student roles. The teacher has determined the outer framework of the dialogue, and will probably decide which suggestions are to be used. The student is helped by the fact that he can review the written dialogue before making the next suggestion, something one can never do in real life.

1.4.3.3   Writing skeleton dialogues
This is a refined form of 'filling in the blanks', and can be done in groups or pairs. If carefully composed, it can give possibilities for selection of appropriate language. It is not role play for the reasons noted in 1.4.3.2 above.

1.4.3.4   Freer dialogue writing in groups
In this case, the students are not limited to the framework of a skeleton dialogue, but can produce their own. Again, there is no immediacy, each utterance can be reviewed before the next is written.

Although the above-mentioned activities are not role play, they can all be used as part of the preparation for role play. How this can be done will be illustrated in following chapters.

Exercises

1   Select one example from each of the three sections (beginners, intermediate, advanced) in the Appendix. Discuss whether they are *role play*, *simulation* or *role play within simulation*.

2   List the roles you usually fulfil in the course of a normal day. For each role note down:
   (a)   The role(s) of the other people you interact with.
   (b)   The level of formality you use with them (on a scale from very formal to very informal).
   (c)   Any special register that the role requires.

3   Think of the function 'inviting people' (in this case to your house for a meal). Write a list of the ways you would express this, from very formal to very informal. For each item on your list provide acceptable and appropriate positive and negative replies.

4   Select a dialogue from a language teaching textbook. Examine it with reference to points 1.2.1 to 1.2.8 above. Is it acceptable, appropriate and natural language? Give reasons for your answer.

Suggestions for further reading[1]

1   On varieties of English, especially formality and politeness see G Leech and J Svartvik (1975) *A Communicative Grammar of English* pp 21–28.

2   For examples of 'asking permission' – formality and role see D A Wilkins (1976) *Notional Syllabuses* pp 59–64.

3   On para-linguistic features see G Brown (1977) *Listening to Spoken English* Chapter 7.

4   On 'turn taking' in conversation see M Coulthard (1977) *An Introduction to Discourse Analysis* pp 52–62. On cultural differences see ibid. pp 48–49.

5   On immediacy of oral interaction see D Crystal and D Davey (1975) *Advanced Conversational English* pp 5 and 8. On appropriateness see ibid. pp 110–111.

6   On teacher-direction see C J Brumfit (1980) *Problems and Principles in Language Teaching* pp 122–129.

7   On role, situation etc. see A Maley and A Duff (1978) *Drama Techniques in Language Learning* pp 1–6.

8   On role-based courses see J P B Allen and S P Corder (1974) *The Edinburgh Course in Applied Linguistics Volume 3* pp 6–7.

9   On register see D A Wilkins (1972) *Linguistics in Language Teaching* pp 136–139.

10   On the difference between role play and simulation see G Sturtridge in K Johnson and K Morrow (1981) *Communication in the Classroom* pp 126–130.

1   All references are to books and articles listed in the Bibliography on pages 93–94.

2 Description and analysis of two role plays

This chapter describes in detail how two role plays were selected, prepared for, organised and executed in the classroom. The first role play is for beginners, the second for advanced students. Each example starts with a description of what happened in the classroom during the actual role play phase.

2.1 Beginners' role play – description

The class of children has had about twenty hours' teaching (though the role play would also be suitable for adults). The classroom has been rearranged so there is plenty of room to move about. There are a few tables placed round the room. Above each is a sign: 'grocer', 'greengrocer', 'butcher' and so on. The signs are nicely decorated and have obviously been made by the students. On the tables are a selection of the goods appropriate to each shop. Sometimes the goods are the 'real thing', sometimes empty packages, sometimes only pictures of the item. Every item is priced. Again, the students seem to have done most of the work. One student stands behind each 'shop' table and the rest of the class move around from 'shop' to 'shop' buying the 'goods'. Toy money changes hands and the bought 'goods' are taken away.

The teacher is standing unobtrusively near the window, near two of the 'shops'. He is ostensibly looking out of the window, but is actually listening carefully, and making mental notes. The 'shopping' goes on for about ten minutes before the class is reassembled.

2.1.1 Examples and comments

What do the students say when they are 'shopping'? What is the teacher listening for? Here are some examples.

Example 1
S1: Hello, I'd like a pound of apples.
S2: Here you are, anything else?
S1: No, thank you.
S2: 40p, please.
S1: Here you are.
S2: Thank you, goodbye.
S1: Goodbye.

This exchange is correct in every detail, and contains only words and phrases previously learned in class. The teacher need not note anything here.

Example 2
S3: Hello, can I help you?
S4: I'd like tea.
S3: How much tea?
S4: A pound.
S3: This tea or this tea?
S4: This tea.
S3: Here you are. Anything else?
S4: A pound of coffee.
S3: Here you are ... (*He hesitates, it seems he has said 'anything else' already. He tries something new.*) ... and more?
S4: No, thank you. How much is that?
S3: £3.50.
S4: Here you are. Goodbye.
S3: Thank you. Goodbye.

This exchange is more interesting as the speakers have tried to experiment a bit. The utterance: 'This tea or this tea?' and: 'This tea' are, from a purely formal grammatical point of view, not strictly correct. The students' gestures were such as to make 'that' the correct determiner in the latter two cases. From a classroom English point of view, however, it is perfectly acceptable at this level, as the meaning is quite clear. It also shows creative thought on the part of the students, as the only time they have encountered 'this' was in the question: 'What's this called in English?'. The 'this/that' distinction has not yet been made in class.

The question: 'and more?' shows a real feeling for the language. Previous lessons had included the phrase: 'and you?' said on a rising intonation, in the following: 'I'm very well, and you?', 'I live in London, and you?'. The word 'more' had not yet occurred formally in the classroom, so it is assumed that S3 had picked it up outside the classroom. As both of these attempts at experimentation were successful, i.e. they were completely understandable if not formally correct, the teacher did not correct the individuals concerned after the role play. Correction of such 'mistakes' may reduce the student's confidence, and curtail further attempts at experimentation.

Example 3
At another 'shop' two students are standing in a 'queue', waiting to be served. They start to talk to each other:

S5: Hello, how are you today?
S6: Fine thanks, and you?
S5: Very well.
    (*Pause*)

S5: How your mother?
S6: He's very well.
    (*Pause*)
S5: It's nice today, isn't it?
S6: Yes it is.

S5 cannot think of a new opening, so the exchange comes to an end. This type of exchange was not included in the role play preparation or instructions, so S5's initiative is to be highly praised, especially at this level.

The question 'How's your mother?' has not yet been formally introduced and practised orally in class, but it has been heard on a listening comprehension tape, so S5 did very well to remember it (although his pronunciation made it barely recognisable!). The teacher makes a note to get S5 to repeat the whole question correctly as soon as possible after the role play.

The teacher also makes a note to do more class work on saying the final 's' in: 'How's', 'He's' etc., as this is a common class error. 'He' and 'she' is also a point for further class work. It could be that S6 did not hear the question clearly, but again it is a general error.

2.2   Beginners' role play – analysis

The casual visitor to this beginners' class might be impressed by the smooth functioning of the role play he saw. What he did not see was the preparation that was done before the class even started on the role play.

2.2.1   Teacher preparation
2.2.1.1   Selection

This is an example of a simple 'survival' role play; students visiting a foreign country will always need to buy things at one time or another. It may be argued that the situation described above is unrealistic as most countries nowadays have supermarkets where you can buy all your foodstuffs without uttering a word. Apart from the fact that this is generally only true of large town supermarkets, many people like going into small speciality shops to buy small amounts of local delicacies for their picnics, etc.

It will also be noted that all the language used in this example can be used in many other survival and shopping situations.

2.2.1.2   Breakdown of roles, functions, etc.
(a) *Situation*: In a shop.
(b) *Roles*: Customer and shop assistant.
(c) *Formality*: Formal.
(d) *Attitudes*: Neutral, polite.
(e) *Language functions*: Asking for goods.
                                     Asking for, and giving, prices.
                                     Asking for, and giving, amounts.

2.2.1.3   Requisite student knowledge
(a) *New material*
Names of common shop goods.
Names of shops selling these.
Names of amounts (half a kilo, etc.).
Names of packaging (a packet, a jar, etc.).
Difference between number and amount (much/many).
The English monetary system.
Polite requests for goods.
The question 'How much/many?'.

(b) *Assumed knowledge*
It is assumed that, before the preparation in 2.2.2 below, the students know:
Numbers to 100.
Greetings ('Good morning', etc.).
'Goodbye'.
'Please', 'thank you', 'here you are'.
A way of asking the 'name' of things in English
(e.g. 'What's this called in English?').
The question 'Can you?' (e.g. 'Can you buy apples at the _____?').

2.2.1.4   Requisite teaching aids
Pictures or realia of common shop goods.
Price tags.
Real or toy English money.
Pictures of the shops to be mentioned.
Role play cards.
A model dialogue.
A dialogue on tape for listening comprehension, which is slightly different from the model dialogue.

2.2.2   Class preparation
2.2.2.1   Linguistic preparation
In this phase, new material is presented and practised; previously learned material is revised.
    Pictures or realia are used to present and practise the new words. A short exchange can be used:

A: What's this called in English?
B: A(n) _____.
A: Thank you.

To begin with the teacher is B and the new words are repeated chorally and individually. The students can then work in pairs with the aids, using the same exchange.
    The new words thus learned can be used again in connection with the

various shops. Pictures of the shops are shown, and the students repeat the names. Students can then ask the teacher:

A: Can you buy _____ at the _____?
B: Yes, that's right/No, at the _____.
A: Thank you.

This short phase also gives factual and cultural information, as the range of goods sold in a particular kind of shop often varies from country to country.

Numbers can be revised, and the new vocabulary already learned consolidated in a phase which presents and practises the English monetary system and amounts. Pictures of goods with price tags and amounts are used in the exchange:

A: How much is tea?
B: £1.00 a pound.
A: Thank you.

After choral and individual repetition, the students can practise in pairs. This exercise is made more realistic if only B is in possession of the prices, so that A is asking because he doesn't know.

2.2.2.2 Linguistic, situational and functional preparation
(a) A dialogue similar to that shown below is presented, and the utterances practised orally (chorally and individually after the teacher or taped model). The aim of this phase is *not* to learn the dialogue by heart. It is purely to get the students to say the utterances with intelligible and acceptable pronunciation, stress, rhythm and intonation.

The word 'intelligible' is used, as at this level it is not realistic to expect a near-native performance. The aim should be a performance which a native speaker (or a reasonably competent non-native speaker) can *understand* without difficulty.

A: Good morning, can I help you?
B: I'd like a pound of tea and half a pound of coffee, please.
A: Here you are, anything else?
B: No, thank you. How much is that?
A: £2.25, please.
B: Here you are.
A: Thank you, goodbye.
B: Goodbye.

(b) Once pronunciation, etc. of the specimen dialogue is intelligible and acceptable, another dialogue or two can be built up on the blackboard or overhead transparency. These dialogues are built up from the teacher's cues and the students' suggestions:

T: Which shop will we go to now?
S: (*e.g.*) The greengrocer's.

T: OK – what does the greengrocer say when you come in?
S: Good afternoon, can I help you? (*T writes on blackboard.*)
T: And what do you say? What do you want to buy?
S: I'd like a pound of tomatoes. (*T writes on blackboard.*)
  (*etc. until the dialogue is finished.*)

In this way the teacher can check the students' understanding of the material, and the students can see how what they have been learning can be rearranged and used to obtain the goods *they* want. The dialogues can also be used for further oral practice (choral, individual, pair).

(c) To give more scope to the role play, 'much' and 'many' can be introduced in the next lesson. A suitable exchange (using visuals) might be:

A: I'd like some _____.
B: How much?/How many?
A: _____ (3, ½ a pound, etc.)
B: Here you are.
A: Thank you.

After the initial class practice, the exchange can be practised in pairs, using the visuals.

(d) This phase is optional. If the students are now producing dialogues reasonably quickly and correctly, it should be left out, or the class will become bored.
  The students work in pairs. Each pair is given a card, for example:

Go into the grocer's and buy three things.
Begin:

A: Good morning, can I help you?
B: I'd like _____.

Write the rest of the dialogue.

These cards can be designed with students of differing abilities in mind.
A pair of 'good' students may merely be told:

Go into the grocer's and buy some things.
Write your dialogue here:

A:
B:

A pair of 'weaker' students may need the extra support of a skeleton dialogue:

> Fill in the blanks in this dialogue:
>
> A: Good _____, can _____?
> B: _____ like _____ and _____. (*etc.*)

When the dialogues have been completed, each pair practises their dialogue orally. Some pairs may then read their dialogue to the rest of the class, accompanying their reading with the handling of the appropriate visuals and money.

(e) If a suitable tape is available, it can now be used for listening comprehension. It will give the better students some idea of how they can expand the situation. A well-made tape will also give practice in listening to English spoken at a natural speed of speech, and add realism to the lesson. The script of the tape used is as follows:

A: Good morning, Mrs MacDonald.
B: Good morning.
A: Lovely day, isn't it?
B: Yes, very warm for April.
A: What can I do for you today?
B: I'd like half a dozen eggs, some bacon . . .
A: Er . . . Danish or English?
B: Danish, I think. About a pound, please, and some strawberry jam.
A: Here you are, anything else?
B: No, thanks, that's all.
A: That'll be £2.11.
B: The price of things! Here you are.
A: Thank you, and here's your change.
B: Goodbye.
A: Goodbye, Mrs MacDonald.

This taped dialogue is used for asking questions on the explicit content (i.e.: 'What did she buy?', 'How much bacon?', 'How many eggs?', 'How much did it cost?'). Short one or two word answers are all that is required. Students should also be asked to guess at the meaning of words they do not know, but which can be inferred from the context, for example: 'What do you think "change" means?'.

(f) A desk is turned into a 'shop'. The students suggest the kind of shop, and select and lay out the relevant goods. A reasonably confident student is given some English money, and is asked to be 'customer' while the teacher is 'shop assistant'. The student has no form of written help. The student buys a few things, goods and money change hands, and the student takes his purchases away.

The activity is repeated, this time with two students.

2.2.3   The role play

Some desks are made into 'shops' as in (f) above, the number depending, of course, on the size of the class. The preparation phases in this example have been so comprehensive that it should not be necessary to give out role cards, even to the 'weaker' students. Students should be given a couple of minutes to write their own shopping list. This should include the shops they will go to, which goods they will buy there, and the amount they need. A few students play 'shop assistants', the rest play 'customers' and the role play is underway.

2.2.4   Follow-up

Immediate follow-up can be done quickly by the teacher asking one or two students what they bought, and how much it cost. Full replies are not necessary, the student need only answer: 'A pound of sugar', 'Three apples', etc.

For subsequent lessons the teacher will work out exercises which practise the general mistakes he noted during the role play.

2.2.5   Further work

(a) Shopping situations can be expanded. The next might be buying clothes. Here the notions of size, colour and material could be introduced: 'I'm looking for a red woollen sweater'.

Souvenir shopping is another obvious example: 'I'm looking for something to take back to my husband'.

At a later point functions other than buying can be included, for example, complaining about faulty goods: 'I'm afraid I have a complaint to make'.

(b) The use of phrases such as: 'I'd like' will be expanded to include other situations and functions, for example, ordering in a café: 'I'd like a cup of tea and a sandwich' or stating wishes to a friend: 'I'd like to go to the cinema tonight'.

2.3   Advanced role play – description

The second class is a class of adults. The class has been divided into two groups, one of six students, one of seven students. As the classroom is quite small, one group is sitting in the corridor. In front of each student is a card on which is written a name and an explanatory note, for example:

Mrs Wilder Parent	or	Miss Johnstone Teacher Primary 1

The names in each group vary, but we see there are two teachers, two or three parents, and a governor of the school. The latter is leading the discussion and making the occasional note. It seems that his job is to direct the discussion and get everyone's opinions. In one group the discussion goes on for 30 minutes, in the other it is still in progress when the classroom time is finished, and the teacher has to stop it as there is another class waiting.

During these discussions the teacher has been sitting in a corner near the door, where he can hear both groups. He has ostensibly been correcting homework, but has in reality been noting down general and particular errors made in the discussions.

2.3.1 Example and comment
Here is a short excerpt from one of the groups:

S1: (*school governor*) And what do you think er, Mrs er, Jones?
S2: My name is Mrs Jones and I have two children in the school, a boy and a girl. And . . . the girl is very . . . doing very badly. Oh! She is so lazy . . . nothing . . . she won't do nothing . . . and I say to her . . . .
S1: Yes, I'm sure you have a problem. Mrs Jones. (*'Mrs Jones'' children exist in real life, and seem to be a bit of a trial; the class is somewhat tired of her twice weekly reports.*) But we are discussing that the school should . . . close down. No in . . . individual problems.
S2: Yes. I mean the . . . it should close down. My children will have better chance with er er more facilities.
S1: Thank you. Do you agree, Mr.Smith?
S3: No, I mean if there is a possible . . .
S4: Possibility.
S3: Possibility to keep the school open . . . we should do it. It's very . . . too far to travel for the young children . . . . The new school is so big . . . er not so friendly . . . .
S4: But wouldn't you agree, Mr Jones . . .

The discussion continues. The teacher has noted that many people in the class are still saying 'I mean' instead of 'I think'. There is also a problem with the use of 'that' – 'we are discussing that'. More work will have to be done, too, on gerund constructions 'a possibility to keep'. On the whole, however, the teacher is pleased with the results of the role play.

2.4 Advanced role play – analysis

2.4.1 Teacher preparation
2.4.1.1 Selection
Most of the students in this class of adults had school age children. It was a class of Danes and there was at the time in Denmark a lot of debate about education: the new elementary school law, the lack of discipline in schools, etc. This was, however, incidental; education is always topical.

The idea for the role play came after the class had begun a series of lessons with 'education' as the theme. There had been a TV programme about the closing down of rural schools the night before a class meeting. This caused some discussion in class, and the subject seemed to engender enough interest for the teacher to judge a follow-up worthwhile.

This does not mean that the teacher should merely hope that a suitable topic for a role play will just crop up, but neither does it mean that a series of lessons should be so rigidly planned that outside influences and the interests of the class cannot be taken into consideration.

2.4.1.2 Breakdown of roles, functions, etc.

(a) *Situation*: A small school in a country village is threatened with closure. It is not economic and has few educational facilities. It is suggested that the students be bussed to a huge new school some 15 miles away. Many parents have protested, and a meeting of parents and teachers is called by the school authorities to discuss the problem.

(b) *Roles*: A school governor (chairperson of the meeting), teachers, parents.

(c) *Formality*: Formal.

(d) *Attitudes*: Here, polite and friendly. If, however, the class has practised other attitudes these could be included, for example a 'parent' might be given this information:

You dislike the county council's attitude to village life and you particularly dislike the school governor.

(e) *Language functions of all roles*:
Ability to put forward point of view politely and clearly, and to 'hold the floor' until this is done.
Ability to agree and disagree politely.
Ability to interrupt politely.

Language functions of chairperson:
Ability to stop/interrupt a speaker politely.
Ability to ask for people's views.
Ability to keep discussion to the point.
Ability to initiate and conclude a discussion.

2.4.1.3 Requisite student knowledge
Knowledge of own, and English educational system.
Names of school subjects and school facilities.
Ways of expressing the language functions listed under 'all roles' above.

It is assumed that before the students embark on the preparation described below, they can formulate themselves clearly and acceptably, if not completely correctly, on topics of general interest.

It is also assumed that they have practised at least some of the language functions mentioned.

2.4.1.4   Requisite teaching aids
No aids are indispensable for this series of lessons, although articles on education from English newspapers and magazines would be relevant, and provide variety, stimulus for discussion, and a more complete grasp of the foreign educational system, and peoples' attitudes to it.

If possible, there should also be a tape for listening comprehension which covers some aspect of the topic.

The type and amount of such material depends very much on the level of the class, and the interest they show in the topic. The teacher should aim at having a wide range of materials available.

2.4.2   Class preparation
At this level the preparation depends very much on the class and its previous knowledge. What is described below is the preparation done for this particular role play with a particular class. Other classes might need more or less preparation, or a different approach entirely.

At this level the students should, as far as possible, be able to direct the development of a series of lessons on a topic. The class activities should be designed so that the students are not 'fed' by the teacher, but do most of the work themselves.

In this instance the topic had been chosen by the class. They had then, in groups, discussed those aspects of education they would most like to cover in class. They decided on the British educational system, discipline in schools, how schools have changed over the years, and the problems facing school leavers. The teacher noted these, and the class was asked to look at pictures, articles, and at their children's school books for material relevant to these aspects, and to bring them to class.

This material, together with that provided by the teacher, was used where relevant. Each lesson was planned from the results of the previous one.

2.4.2.1   Linguistic, factual and cultural preparation
(a) *New vocabulary*. As not all the vocabulary was new to all the students, the teacher let the students think of the necessary words first, and only provided a word when none of the students knew it.

The students 'interviewed' the teacher about the British educational system. Students had been asked to come with questions. Where the students missed a point that the teacher thought was important to their understanding of the system, he cued a suitable question, 'Ask me about . . .'.

A summary of the answers was built up on the blackboard. Students were then asked, in pairs, to make up a similar summary for their own country, noting the similarities and differences. This was also put up on the blackboard.

(b) *New functions*. The only *new* function here was 'interrupting politely'. Ways of doing this were noted and practised: 'If I may come in here . . .?', 'Do you mind if I just . . .?', 'Er . . . er . . . er . . .' (until speaker takes notice), etc.

The teacher then started making definite statements about some of the facts noted on the blackboard: 'I think it is much better for children to start school at five . . .', etc. Students were asked to interrupt politely at suitable points, either to add further comment, or to agree or disagree.

(c) *Consolidation and revision.* The technique of making statements, interrupting, etc. described above, was done by the students in class, then in pairs. This consolidated the new function and revised old functions, i.e. giving opinions, etc.

(d) *Further practice.* A letter to an English newspaper about the lack of discipline in today's schools was given to the students to read at home. They were also asked to think about their own opinions on discipline in schools, and in what ways schools had changed since they were children.

At the next class, groups were formed to discuss these topics, using the following questions:

Do you agree with the letter writer?
Why or why not?
What about the discipline in Danish schools – is there too little today? Give examples if possible.
How have schools changed since you were young? (Think also of buildings, facilities, etc.)
Which of these changes do you think are good, which bad?

Groups were asked to practise interrupting, agreeing and disagreeing during the course of the group work, and to make short notes of the group's opinions.

Each group then reported its opinions briefly to the class and a general discussion took place. It was during this discussion that the TV broadcast about the closure of rural schools was mentioned and commented on. For the next meeting the class was asked to think about the advantages and disadvantages of closing rural schools.

2.4.2.2 Situational preparation

The theme of the role play was explained to the class. The students then built up the situation themselves, and the information was noted on the blackboard. What they decided is shown on the table overleaf.

SMALL SCHOOL *<distance 20 km>* LARGE SCHOOL

Built 1923	Built 1978
90 students	600 students
Five rooms	Fifty rooms (including cookery, woodwork, art rooms, etc.)
No special facilities except school garden where children grow vegetables, etc.	All newest equipment including swimming pool. No school garden.
Used nightly for evening classes, and all other community activities.	Used nightly for evening classes. Not used for other community activities.

2.4.2.3   Role preparation
Students prepared their roles in pairs. The role cards gave the following information:

Role 1

You are parents of children at the old school. Decide whether you are for or against the move, and list your arguments. Be prepared to put your opinion clearly and politely, and to counter any arguments against it.

Role 2

You are teachers at the old school. Decide whether you are for or against the move, and list your arguments. Be prepared to give your opinion clearly and politely, and to counter any arguments against it.

Role 3

You are the school governor. You must chair the meeting. You must make sure that everyone's views are heard. You yourself are for the move, but must appear to remain neutral. Remember to 'open' and 'close' the meeting.

The students were allowed to make notes during their preparation, and to call on the teacher for help. The two students preparing the role of school governor were given a little extra help with the more official side of their role, for example, they will need to know phrases for 'opening' and 'closing' a meeting, as stated in their role cards. Each pair was numbered A and B, and after about 15 minutes' preparation all the A's formed one group, and all the B's formed another, making two 'meetings'. One younger student decided to be a pupil at the old school, and prepared alone. She joined group B.

2.4.3 The role play

The two meetings were arranged; one, as already mentioned, in the corridor. The teacher had instructed the 'school governors' to start the meetings by introducing themselves and the other participants.

No time for finishing was set, but when the chairpersons thought that everyone had had a fair chance to express their opinions, and to discuss those of others, they could bring the meetings to a close, drawing any conclusions that might have come out of it.

2.4.4 Follow-up

Each group was asked to give the general feeling of the meeting. Group A, who had finished first, had felt that the old school should be kept open, as it was important for the community as a whole, and also important for the children to feel themselves part of a community, rather than be isolated in a large and impersonal educational 'ghetto'. The suggestion was made that the money which would otherwise be spent on transport to the new school could be used to make improvements to the old school.

The second group had not got so far, their chairperson was a little too vague, and let the discussion 'wander' from the point. Most people, however, seemed to be for the move.

There was no class discussion after these reports, it was obvious that the students felt the topic to be finished. One or two students commented on the role play as such. One criticism was that they were not sure whether they were discussing a Danish or an English school. We agreed that this should have been made clear from the start. Some others felt that they would have preferred to be *given* an opinion in their role play cards. However there was not general agreement on this.

2.4.5 Further work

The topic 'education' continued with a discussion of language learning in the state school system, and in their own evening class.

The errors the teacher had noted during the role play were used for formal class work, particularly work on gerund constructions.

The 'discussion functions' already learned were revised and expanded in work with subsequent topics. The next topic the students had chosen was 'alternative energy sources'.

Exercises

The two examples in this chapter were for beginners' and advanced classes. Look at these role cards for a role play for an intermediate class:

Role 1

Phone up _____. Ask how he/she is. Comment on the weather (it is raining). Invite _____ for dinner at the weekend. Find a suitable day. You have a new address, so tell _____ how to get there.

Role 2

_____ phones you up. You are well. It is raining. You would like to have dinner with _____. You are going to the theatre on Friday. _____ has just moved to a new house. Ask him/her how to get there.

---

1 List the functions the students will need before they can tackle this role play.

2 What roles are involved? (What is the relationship between Role 1 and Role 2?)

3 What will the level of formality be? What attitudes will Role 1 and Role 2 have?

4 Using language that is acceptable and appropriate (keep the answers to questions 1 to 3 in mind), write down the kind of conversation that these cards might produce.

5 Take one of the functions from question 1 and, assuming it to be new material, sketch out how you would present and practise it.

3 The advantages and disadvantages of role play

The two role plays described in the previous chapter were successful, both from the teacher's and the students' point of view. This does not mean that all role plays attempted by those particular classes were successful, or that role play is a teaching/learning technique which has no drawbacks. Many readers will already have worked out what role play would mean in their own classes, and what problems they will be likely to meet. Others, who have tried role play, will already have met these problems.

This chapter analyses the main advantages and disadvantages of using role play in the language classroom, and hopes to show that the former far outweigh the latter.

3.1 Advantages

3.1.1 Maximum student activity
For role play to be fully successful, each student should be active almost 100% of the time.

It may be argued that, in the examples in Chapter two, only one student, the one who is speaking, is active at any given moment. This is not true.

Much confusion has been caused by the arbitrary division of language skills into 'active skills' (speaking and writing) and 'passive skills' (listening and reading), as though activity were measured by bodily activity and sound alone.

The amount of activity required from a participant in a normal conversational situation has already been discussed. Coherent speech requires a great deal of mental activity, both in its formulation, in the monitoring of other's reception of it, and in its possible subsequent adaptation in the light of that monitoring.

The listener must show understanding or otherwise of the speaker, relate what is being said to his own opinions and needs in order to be able, when he has judged that his turn to speak has come, to formulate an appropriate, acceptable and understandable message.

Few classroom activities require the high level of mental activity suggested above. Oral exercises ('drills', 'pattern practice', 'pair practice', etc.) and most forms of group work, have a set, predictable pattern.

During these activities the student, when not actually speaking, need not give his full attention to the exercise. If his attention wanders the 'action' will not be radically held up, as the teacher or other students will call him to task, or ask another student to continue while he again turns his concentration to the exercise. If he makes a mistake he will be stopped and given time to reconsider and re-formulate his utterance, or merely be asked to repeat the correct version.

Usually the language he is required to produce is, if not totally predictable, then at least limited to a narrow range of options, and can be produced reasonably quickly and correctly without a great deal of thought.

In most cases such activities are teacher-directed, so that the student, instead of having to use his own judgement, has an authority to appeal to.

None of these features is present in real life conversation, so these activities do not practise everything the student will need outside the classroom. Role play does. This is not to say that such exercises/activities are valueless. I believe them to be an essential part of language learning. It does mean, however, that if they are to be of maximum use to the student, the language they practise must be extended and developed through role play.

3.1.2 Relevance, interest and discipline

Teachers of schoolchildren have discipline problems. This has always been true, but these problems seem to have been increasing in recent years. Teachers who have such problems may well feel that role plays such as the shopping example, where the students are out of their seats, going from 'shop' to 'shop', are not, from a discipline point of view, a good idea. If a class is unruly when seated, the situation is likely to become chaotic if the students are permitted to wander 'at will' round the classroom. It is not within the scope of this book to discuss in detail the possible reasons for lack of class discipline, but it is relevant to note those points appertaining to discipline and role play.

Quite often schoolchildren cannot understand why they are required to learn certain things. The subject and the learning aim have been chosen by the school authorities, and may seem to be totally unconnected to the students' present needs and experiences. Even when the aim is reasonably clear, as, for example, learning English in Scandinavia (where it is almost a second language, and even the youngest children cannot avoid coming into contact with it through the mass media) then the activities and exercises the students are required to do in class may not seem in any way relevant to that aim.

An extreme, but very common example of this is reading aloud. In a class of, say, thirty students, if all thirty, or only half the class, have to read aloud one or two sentences, then only one student is active at any given moment. The rest of the class need not listen, they have the text in front of them. Having once read, the student knows that he is unlikely to be asked to do anything else for some time, and can therefore think of other things. Probably the only time this activity will be of any use is in an examination sometime in the future. It does not seem to be relevant to their daily lives, or help them with any contact they may have with the language outside the classroom. It is not unreasonable, therefore, that children become bored and restless during such exercises.

There are, of course, other exercises which are more interesting and require more activity on the part of the student, but many of these are again teacher-directed, and their long-term relevance is often not immediately obvious.

The relevance of a role play which has been chosen to suit the students' interests, experience and needs *is* obvious. It also gives the student a chance to use the language *himself*, without the direct control of the teacher. No student who is interested in what he is doing will misbehave. Activity and discipline are also closely linked. It is not natural for children to sit quietly and still for long periods of time. Many language learning exercises require the student to do just that – sit still. If the lesson is not one of the first of the day there are two possible results of this; an undisciplined class or a class of students whose minds are on other things, and are therefore very quiet. In either case the effectiveness of teaching and learning will not be high.

An exercise which is not only seen to be relevant, but also requires mental *and* bodily activity, will freshen concentration and interest, thus increasing the possibility of effective learning.

Adults do not usually cause discipline problems. They have a greater experience and understanding of education. This means they can look at learning from a more abstract point of view, and will therefore accept a lot of work which does not seem to be of immediate relevance to their ultimate aim.

But for any age group, aim or type of class, whether it is voluntary or compulsory, every student responds positively to activities which have an obvious practical application. A feeling that what one is doing is relevant and useful is a powerful factor in increasing the motivation to learn; increased motivation leads to increased student involvement in the learning process.

3.1.3 Mixed ability groups

As no learning group is homogenous, teachers are always in need of activities that can be graded to suit a wide range of abilities. Role play is an excellent exercise for dealing with this problem and can be graded in a number of ways.

(a) Roles can be designed with 'faster' or 'slower' students in mind. In the advanced example in Chapter two, it is obvious that the 'school governor' has the most difficult role. He has not only to concentrate on what is being said, and give his own comments, but also to make sure everyone gets a chance to speak, to 'open' and 'close' the meeting, and to make sure it runs smoothly. This is a role for a student who is fairly fluent and confident, not one who has to concentrate closely on every utterance in order to follow the discussion.

This type of 'responsible' role is also good for a student who is very dominant in other class activities, the type who knows all the answers, and talks whenever he gets the chance. Giving such a student a major role will often satisfy his need to make his presence felt, and he will use much of his energy in fulfilling the role as well as possible, becoming, as a result, less obtrusive.

The shyer student can also be catered for. Had there, in that advanced group, been a rather shy and quiet student, then a role as secretary could have been created. The secretary could have taken short notes of the meeting, which could later have been used to formulate the group report. (This role is only possible, of course, if the student concerned has the required command of writing skills.) I do not believe that a student who is by nature a quiet person should be required to do as much talking as the others. If he does not say much in his mother tongue, then there is little point in trying to make him a chatterbox in the foreign language. The task of the teacher is to improve performance in the foreign language, not alter personality.

Roles, then, can be created to fit not only the linguistic ability, but also the personality of the individual student.

(b) Role descriptions can be altered to suit varying abilities. In a role play where the roles require more or less the same type and amount of student activity from each student, as in the 'shopping' example, then the students can be given guidance according to ability. If the teacher had judged it necessary to give out role play cards for this role play, they might have looked like this:

Role 1 – card for 'slow' student

Fill in what you want to buy.
You want to buy:

_____ at the grocer's.
_____ and _____ at the greengrocer's.
_____ at the butcher's.

Remember to say: 'I'd like . . .' and 'Thank you'.

Role 1 – card for 'fast' student

Buy things at three shops.
Make a list of what you want first.

Similarly, in the advanced example, all the 'parents' have the same type of role, but these too can be rewritten to suit varying abilities and situations:

Role 2 – card for 'slow' student

You are a parent with children at the school. (How many? How old are they?) Decide if you are for or against the move. Note down your arguments. Be prepared to give your opinions clearly and politely. Remember to use phrases like:

In my opinion . . .
I think . . .

Try to agree or disagree with what the other people say, remember phrases like:

I agree entirely . . .
I'm not sure I agree. I think . . .

Role 2 – card for 'fast' student

You are a parent with children at the school. Decide whether you are for or against the move, and be prepared to give your opinion clearly and politely, and to counter any arguments against it.

When designing role cards of this type, the teacher should be careful not to give a slow student so much help that the student has no possibility of choosing his own language. This would make the exercise guided dialogue work, not role play.

(c) Another possibility is to have students of mixed abilities prepare roles together. In the advanced example, a 'slower' student could prepare the role with a 'faster' student (in which case only the role card for the 'fast' student would be given out). The 'slower' student could make more detailed notes while the preparation was taking place so that he had some support when in the actual role play situation. Students are often willing to help each other in this way, especially in smaller groups, and should be encouraged to do so.

(d) Alternately, students of similar abilities can prepare roles together, and the amount of time given to groups for role preparation can vary. 'Slower' students might be given the role card for the 'slow' student and, say, twenty minutes' preparation time. 'Faster' students might spend ten minutes of this time on another role play-related exercise, and the final ten minutes on preparation (using the role card for the 'fast' student above).

After a little practice in the composition of role plays, teachers will find that there are many ways of relating role cards and role preparation to the abilities of the individual students.

3.2 Disadvantages

If the main aim of the class is oral/aural proficiency, then it is difficult, from a pedagogical point of view, to find any disadvantages in using role play as a teaching and learning technique. But there is no doubt that in certain classes, and in certain teaching situations, there may well be some practical drawbacks.

3.2.1 Organisation

Few teachers operate in ideal circumstances. The majority work in classrooms which are too small, and with classes which are, numerically, too large. Often the furniture is bolted to the floor, and equipment other than books and a blackboard almost non-existent. Role play may therefore be difficult from a purely practical point of view. It is useless to suggest that role play groups be placed in extra rooms and corridors if these are not available. Similarly, the noise level produced by a class of forty, divided into eight role play groups in a small classroom, may be so high as to make concentration impossible.

There is little the teacher can do about such problems except choose or design role plays which will adapt to his particular situation. The short 'interview' situations in Chapter six, for example, can be done without the students leaving their seats. Perhaps two or three role play groups can be arranged, and the rest of the class given another, quieter task. I have even seen a successful role play based on 'asking and telling the way' done in a class where the furniture could not be moved. The aisles between the desks were 'streets' and each desk was a 'building' (town hall, bank, etc.), each 'building' being indicated by pictures.

With care in selection, and a little imagination, many practical problems are not insurmountable.

3.2.2 Time

If the time taken for preparation and follow-up work is included, then role play will take up a lot of classroom time. The beginners' example in Chapter two takes at least four classroom hours; the advanced example took eight classroom hours. Neither is it possible to predict how much time will be needed, especially for the role play itself. An advanced group of mine, involved in a 'Bellcrest story'[1] business role simulation, started one hour before the end of the class time. When I left an hour later to teach another class, they were still far from finished, and continued for another three-quarters of an hour.

1   J Webb *The Bellcrest Story* (OUP 1973).

Some teachers, especially those who teach classes which lead up to examinations, and therefore have a set syllabus to keep in mind, will argue that it is not possible to spend that amount of time on one activity. Their classes will fall behind with the syllabus, and thus fail their examinations.

This is a valid argument if the aim of your class is, say, proficiency in the written language, accurate translation, or reading the classics. In general, though, the increasing tendency nowadays both for school classes and evening classes, is to have oral proficiency as their aim. Even Ministry of Education circulars dealing with aims and syllabuses abound with phrases like 'communicative competence', 'functional language skills', 'oral fluency'. If these are our aims, then any time spent on an activity which will achieve these aims is surely wisely spent.

Role play does not exist by itself. A look at the preparation phases for the two examples in Chapter two will show that all language skills are involved; understanding, speaking, reading and writing. If it is felt that the class needs extra practice in any one of these, then this can be taken into consideration when the role play is being planned, and can form a greater part of the preparation or follow-up phase. Extra writing practice could have been provided, for example, in the advanced role play, by getting the students to write letters expressing different points of view to the local paper, or by asking each group to write a formal report of their discussion. The question is not so much whether we can afford to spend time on role play, but whether we can afford *not* to.

3.3 Further points for consideration

Two points which can be described neither as advantages or disadvantages of role play, but which have both positive and negative aspects are:

(a) The problem of the teacher's and the students' attitude towards role play and other related forms of freer classroom work.

(b) The problem of mistakes.

These are discussed below.

3.3.1 The teacher's new role

In most role plays the teacher will not take part. If he does, it will not be in his role as teacher. The teacher's role during the role play phase is to be as unobtrusive as possible. There are two ways in which this can be done. The first is as described in the two examples in Chapter two, where the teacher either sits somewhere where he can hear much of what is going on, (as in the advanced example); or, when the role play requires a lot of moving around on the part of the students, as in the beginners' example, the teacher can move quietly round the room. Where there is a large class, with a lot of role play groups, or where the groups are in corridors or other rooms, tape recorders can be used.

The second way in which the teacher can observe the role play is by taking a role himself. This should not be a major role, or the teacher may quickly become the dominating personality, and the role play will turn into something resembling teacher-guided group work. Minor roles, which nevertheless give the teacher a chance to be near the 'action', are, for example, a porter, a head waiter, a secretary.

With classes used to role play, and used to discussing teaching techniques and their aims, these subterfuges may not be necessary. Such classes are well aware of what is happening and acknowledge the 'rules' of the whole language learning game. They will therefore not be self-conscious or inhibited if the teacher is *seen* making notes. They may not even notice it.

The advantage of the teacher's new role, either as observer or minor player, is that he is freed from the task of running and organising the class. A well planned, well prepared role play runs itself. The teacher is therefore free to listen for mistakes, misunderstandings and problems. From these he can evaluate the effectiveness of his teaching, and decide if further work on certain points is necessary. Role play is the nearest he can come *in the classroom* to being able to watch his students perform in the foreign language environment.

3.3.2   The teacher's and student's attitudes

Most teachers have definite attitudes towards classroom management and discipline. They know how they want their students to behave towards them, the teacher, towards the classroom activities the subject requires, and towards their fellow students. Teachers who are considering the use of role play as one of their regular teaching procedures may worry about the discipline problems that may crop up (see 3.1.2 above). A much greater, psychological problem for many teachers is the fact that role play requires, not only in the actual role play phase, but also in many of the preparation phases, a lessening of the traditional authority and classroom dominance of the teacher. For role play to be of maximum effectiveness it must be accompanied by a more open approach to teaching and learning. This is manifested in many ways:

(a) Greater student involvement in the choice of materials and learning activities. Students should be encouraged to suggest topics and ideas for class and group work, and to discuss which activities they enjoy and find of most use.

(b) The use of more 'open-ended' exercises, i.e. the replacing of mechanical stimulus/response drills with exercises which more closely resemble real communication.

(c) More exercises and activities which require that the students work in groups or pairs, with the minimum of teacher direction.[1]

1   (b) and (c) are discussed in detail in Chapter five.

(d) Less formal classroom arrangement and management. You cannot have a conversation with the back of your companion's head. Wherever the furnishings of the classroom allow, students should be able to look at each other, if not in one large group, then in several smaller groups. Similarly, it is very difficult to speak naturally if every utterance must be preceded by the speaker raising his hand, or standing up.

Even though the teacher is prepared to adopt, or has, wholly or partly, adopted this more open attitude, there may still be problems.

Children may respond eagerly to such changes, but their parents may feel that they show a lack of respect, or an undesirable tendency towards lack of discipline, and therefore a lack of effective learning.

Teachers of adults may find that their students, who have usually been brought up in a rigid classroom tradition, have fixed views on 'good' classroom practice. 'Good' classroom practice usually means that the teacher is the undisputed authority, and 'real' learning can only take place under his direct control. Teachers faced with these problems should be careful to make their students and/or their parents aware of *why* the approach has been changed. They should also be careful to introduce changes gradually, e.g. short bouts of simple pair work and group work before extensive group work, short interview situations before full-scale role plays. If all the changes take place at once, students will become confused and uncertain, and may long for the security of the old system.

3.3.3 Mistakes

Role play is an exercise which gives the student freedom to select and use his own language and accompanying para-linguistic and extra-linguistic behaviour, without the interference or guidance of the teacher. As the student is not yet proficient in the foreign language, it is obvious that students will make mistakes in the execution of such an exercise.

The nature of the activity means that there is a possibility of making mistakes across the full range of the linguistic spectrum: mistakes in structure, lexis, phonology; mistakes in para-linguistic and extra-linguistic features; mistakes in formality and attitude. Sometimes these mistakes will lead to the formulation of utterances which are unacceptable or inappropriate within the given situation.

Mistakes will be made during role plays, no matter how carefully prepared, and, due to the nature of the exercise, they cannot be corrected immediately. To many teachers, especially those trained in a language teaching method based on behaviourism, this is heresy.

During formal language work, whether based on behaviouristic principles or not, the aim is that the language being practised should be as formally correct as possible. The student's choices are very limited. This limitation of choice means it is difficult for the teacher to be sure that the correct utterance or response is being made because the student knows *why* it is correct. Correct responses may be made for other reasons:

(a) The exercises have been so designed as to leave no possibility of making a mistake (as in mechanical stimulus/response drills).

(b) The student may be reacting to cues given, consciously or unconsciously, by the teacher. If the teacher frowns, the answer must be in some way wrong; if he smiles, it is probably correct. Each teacher has his own, very subtle, cues. These cues may be helpful in a formal, controlled exercise, but the teacher cannot *always* be around to guide the student in this way.

(c) It may be clear to the student why the response is correct within the framework of that particular exercise, but this does not mean that he understands how it relates to the total linguistic picture he has formed up to date.

If, then, only formal, teacher-controlled exercises are used in the classroom, the teacher cannot be sure that the student can select and use the correct language when the teacher or the textbook is not in control. By giving students freedom in the classroom to try out and experiment with the language on their own, we can find out how much of what they have learned they understand how to use. Any mistakes made can be analysed by the teacher and used as a basis for further exercises.

The relaxation of teacher control in role play means that the teacher has a chance in the classroom of discovering, and eventually correcting, mistakes and misconceptions, thus minimising the possibility of the same mistakes being made outside the classroom, where they may cause misunderstanding, or even embarrassment between the student and his interlocuter.

It should be quite clear that I am not *condoning* the making of mistakes; role play should be carefully prepared so that the students have the linguistic tools necessary to cope with the task. But to attempt, as some behaviourists do, to avoid making mistakes, is impossible unless we limit the language the students produce to such an extent that they are merely parroting the teacher. To suggest that mistakes not immediately corrected will be ineradicable at a later date is to suggest that, by some strange process, we can learn, and never forget, an incorrect utterance made once or twice, while we find it so difficult to remember a correct utterance that we must practise it in numerous exercises!

Discussion

1   What do you feel your role as teacher is? What type of role do your students want/expect you to play?
2   How would you characterise a well-disciplined class?
3   What are the aims of the classes you teach or are preparing to teach? (The official aims laid down by educational authorities and/or the students' own aims.) Do you think role play will help you achieve these aims? Give reasons for your answers.

Exercises

1   Select a set of role play cards from the examples in the Appendix (or elsewhere). Rewrite the cards to suit:

  (a) Slower students.
  (b) Faster students.

2   Sketch out a number of role play situations which would interest the following classes learning English for general purposes:

  (a) Children. (Choose your own level and age range.)
  (b) Mixed adults.

Suggestions for further reading

1   On mistakes see J Dakin (1973) *The Language Laboratory and Language Learning* pp 14–15 and page 29, D A Wilkins (1972) *Linguistics in Language Teaching* pp 173–174 and D A Wilkins (1974) *Second-language Learning and Teaching* page 37.

2   On behaviourism see D A Wilkins (1972) *Linguistics in Language Teaching* pp 161–168.

3   On furniture see J Rogers (1977) *Adults Learning* pp 101–105 and A Maley and A Duff (1978) *Drama Techniques in Language Learning* pp 14–15.

4   On the teacher's role in role play see J Rogers (1977) *Adults Learning* pp 152–153.

5   On the advantages of role play see J Revel (1979) *Teaching Techniques for Communicative English* pp 60–63.

4 A role play checklist

Before embarking on role playing in class, it is essential that all aspects of the activity have been carefully considered by the teacher, and that the role play itself has been carefully prepared for in class. This chapter analyses how this can be done. It can therefore be used as a checklist for the teacher, not only before the role play, but also after its completion, to find the reasons for its success (or lack of it!).

The number of points listed below is long, and having to keep them in mind may seem to make the preparation of role play a formidably complex process, but the various divisions have been made mainly from the point of view of organisation. In practice one area often overlaps another, or several other areas.

For example, it may be found that the situational and cultural preparation can be naturally included in the linguistic preparation. Such overlapping is to be desired, as it helps to show how closely all aspects of a language are linked together.

Careful consideration of the points in this chapter will not guarantee a successful role play, but it will help to avoid the worst pitfalls, and produce encouraging results from early attempts at role play.

4.1 Selection

A role play cannot be successful unless it has been chosen with the level, needs and interests of the students in mind.

4.1.1 Level
Any role play should form an integral part of the logical progression of a class's course plan. The teacher must assess what the role play requires with regard to linguistic competence, cultural and situational understanding, and so on. If there is too great a gap between this and the student's present competence in the language, then the role play should be left until the class is nearer the level required, or, if it is possible, simplified to suit the present level of the class. Preparation for role play will of course, require the assimilation of *some* new material. Only the individual teacher can judge how much new material it is reasonable to expect the class to learn before a role play.

It is obvious that the beginners' class who did the shopping role play in Chapter two would be incapable of coping with the advanced example in that chapter, but the problem can often be more subtle than this. The teacher must keep in mind *all* of the features of oral communication when assessing the level and suitability of a role play.

For example, I once watched a very well planned lesson for a beginners' class. Role play was the transfer phase. The lesson started with a model dialogue of a shopping situation:

A: Can I help you?
B: Yes, I'm looking for a blouse.
A: Size?
B: 36.
A: And what colour?
B: White.
A: How about this one?
B: That's nice; may I try it on?

The dialogue was developed in the practice phase to include asking about price (this was revision of previously learned language), and talking about material (cotton, wool, etc.). Materials had also been mentioned in previous lessons.

The teacher had then felt that the students had spent so much time practising 'buying clothes' that a role play similar to the formal exercises would be boring. He had therefore developed a role play with the same situation and roles, but with an entirely different *function*, that of returning goods. The role cards said:

Role 1 – customer

You bought a blouse yesterday. You do not like it now. Take it back to the shop and change it or get your money back.

Role 2 – shop assistant

The customer wants to change what he/she bought, or he/she wants his/her money back. Help him/her.

This class had never learned the function of returning goods, and the preparation they had done had not prepared them for the type of language they would need here. They would not know how to explain why they no longer liked the garment, neither would they know how to arrange getting and giving the money back.

Such a role play might not bore the students, but it would certainly frustrate them.

The role play should suit the level of the class, and be closely connected with the work immediately preceding it.

4.1.2   The students' needs

Why are the students learning the language? If they intend to visit, as a tourist, a country where the foreign language is spoken, then role plays based on tourist situations (asking for directions, travel information, etc.) are an obvious choice. This type of role play is usually chosen for most beginners' classes anyway, as the more concrete type of language they require (asking and answering about *facts*: price, time, distance, place, etc.) is the type of language the students can reasonably be expected to understand and learn at this level.

At the higher levels, however, tourist role plays, no matter how complex they are made, are limiting and will eventually become boring. At these levels, with classes learning English for general purposes, it is difficult to know exactly what they will be required to, or want to, use the language for. We must therefore try to select role plays that will give the students an opportunity to practise a wide range of vocabulary, functions and attitudes.

Therefore, while it can be argued that the advanced class in Chapter two will never need to fulfil the role of parent or teacher in English, it may be assumed that, during contact with speakers of the language, it is likely that they will have to express opinions, agree, disagree, etc. This is what the role *play* has helped them to do.

Similarly, in a tourist situation, few students will have to fulfil the role of policeman. If the policeman is giving directions: 'It's the second turning on your right', then the function and the language is useful. But if the role play requires the policeman to arrest someone: 'Anything you say will be taken down . . .', then the student is being asked to practise a function and language which would only be needed by a policeman intending to work in the foreign language environment.

If it does happen that a role play requires a student to use language which is not compatible with his predicted needs (e.g. the leader of a formal meeting may need 'meeting' language), then the student concerned can be given more detail on his role card and be told which phrases or words to use. During the preparation phase the teacher can give that student extra help. On the whole, though, roles which require a lot of such specialised language which will be of little practical use to the student should be avoided.

4.1.3   The students' interests

A role play which does not interest the students will not be a success.

One way to ensure interest is for the students to be allowed to choose the topic or situation themselves. The amount of freedom given in this choice depends on the level of the class. At the lower levels the class might be allowed to select from a number of teacher-determined suggestions. Students at the higher levels might select a list of topics or themes they are interested in, and, with the teacher's guidance, select how they might work with these. This approach means some extra work on the part of the teacher, for it is almost impossible to plan more than one or two lessons ahead. Also, the class might select a theme for which there is no ready-made role play available, thus placing most of the burden of designing a suitable one on the teacher.

While the approach outlined above is to be preferred, teachers inexperienced in role play techniques, or classes unused to being asked to think for themselves, will find it easier initially to work with pre-selected materials.

The age of the students should be considered. Pre-teenage children are not likely to be interested in a formal dinner party role play. Adults are hardly likely to be interested in planning a school discotheque evening.

The students' daily life and free-time interests are also relevant. A class mainly composed of parents with school-age children is more likely to be interested in the problem of closing down small schools, than is a class of younger students.

4.1.4 The students' experience
This is, of course, closely linked with 4.1.3 above.

When the use of role play in the language learning classroom began to be seriously discussed, I was asked to demonstrate the technique to a group of teachers. The only class I had tried role play with was a class of business people, and as this had been a success I decided to demonstrate one of the business examples. The demonstration was a failure.

This time the roles were being played by teachers, not business people. Although they had the formal linguistic ability to cope with the situation, they did not have the necessary experience of the business world, and so were unable to relate to the situation. Now when demonstrating role play to a group of teachers, I usually use a situation built up around a fictional language school, and the allocation of a sum of money for equipment. This is always a great success as the situation, roles and language are within the participants' own field of experience.

4.2 Preparation

4.2.1 The teacher's pre-class preparation
Once the teacher has selected a role play suitable for his particular class, it is necessary for him to assess what class work will have to be done prior to the role play phase.

Four areas are discussed below. As has already been mentioned, the more closely these are linked in the preparation activities, the better. The students should experience language as an integrated whole, not as a series of seemingly unrelated items to be learned.

4.2.1.1 Linguistic preparation
Accurate prediction of what language the student will need, or indeed want to use in any particular role or situation becomes more difficult the higher

the level. The language needed for simple tourist situations (e.g. asking about train times and ticket prices at the station), is almost totally predictable; the arguments a student might put forward for, say, re-directing the route of a proposed motorway, are not.

Some prediction is possible. If 'traffic problems' is the theme of the series of lessons, then it can be reasonably assumed that words like 'public transport' and 'traffic jam' will be needed. They can therefore be introduced and practised. As this theme is developed into a role play, the subject of which is the improvement of traffic conditions in a town, the function of 'giving opinions' will be needed: 'In my opinion (public transport should be free of charge)'. Ways of expressing this function can also be formally practised.

Apart from formal practice of the more predictable items, our overall aim should be to build up the students' command of a set of general linguistic tools, and, by using these in different types of activities, make the student aware of how they can be used and recombined to suit a wide variety of situations and roles.

Let us consider, for example, the phrase: 'I'd like . . .' . This will probably be learned first as an expression of the function 'making polite requests'. For this function it can be used in many situations, for example:

I'd like a pound of apples. (*shop*)
I'd like a cup of coffee. (*café*)
I'd like a double room. (*hotel*)
I'd like some information. (*e.g. station*)
(*etc.*)

'I'd like' can also be used to express different functions:
I'd like a pound of apples. (*request*)
I'd like to see the new film at the Ritz. (*wish*)
I'd like to say that . . . (*stating opinion*)
I'd like an explanation . . . (*complaining*)

We can say the same thing in different ways. 'I'd like an explanation' can be said in such a way as to mean:

(a) I may be stupid and not understand, or someone may have made a mistake, but I am sure we can clear it up.

(b) I am most annoyed about this, and if I do not get a suitable explanation I will complain to the manager.

Good introduction and explanation by the teacher, and extensive oral production in the form of repetition, oral exercises, pair work, group work and role play, is in itself not sufficient to give the students a real 'feel' for the language. It is also necessary to provide a wide exposure to different kinds of spoken and written English through the use of authentic tapes and text materials.

4.2.1.2 Situational and cultural preparation

A situation which appears to be superficially the same in two linguistic or cultural areas may, in fact, be fundamentally different.

In Chapter two it was mentioned that shops sell different goods in different countries. For example, almost every grocer and tobacconist in Denmark sells several kinds of beer, and usually a selection of wines and spirits. In Sweden, only a few minutes away by ferry, if you wish to buy anything other than light beer, you must look closely for the nearest state liquor store. In Britain, outside pub opening hours, you must look for the magic word 'licensed'. Other examples of cultural differences are tipping, and dress in religious buildings.

The above examples may be quite easily learned, as they deal with fact, but it may be more difficult when the differences deal with built-in, automatic behaviour and language.

Greeting people is an excellent example. There are several aspects that must be taken into consideration: the situation (informal party, business meeting, etc.), the level of formality between the participants (strangers, friends, etc.), the language to be used, the actions involved, and even the distance between people.

If, in Denmark, I meet someone by chance in the street who I know reasonably well, and meet sometimes on a social or professional level, we shake hands. If I know them socially, it is quite likely one of us will say: 'Tak for sidst' (i.e. 'Thank you for the last time we met'), even if this was some considerable time ago! Meeting someone in similar circumstances in Britain, it is unlikely we would shake hands, or thank each other for previous meetings.

Differences of this type can be explained, but a greater understanding is reached by using audio-visual material for discussion and analysis. Exposure to natural taped material enabling the students to listen to people speaking to each other in different roles and situations has already been mentioned. Picture material can also be used:

In this series of pictures[1] the point about different ways of greeting people in different cultures is admirably illustrated. Such pictures can lead to a discussion of how the same situation is approached in the students' own culture, and this can then be compared to Britain or other English-speaking countries.

Awareness of the differences is not enough. The 'English' way of doing things must be practised formally, and in freer situations until it becomes *automatic* behaviour for the student. It can be seen that role play is an excellent exercise for this purpose.

4.2.1.3 Factual preparation

Apart from the cultural 'facts' described above, the participants in a role play must be in possession of more concrete facts before they can play their role with confidence.

In a beginners' role play where a student is asking for information at a railway station, the person giving the information must be in possession of the relevant facts: the times of the trains, prices of tickets, etc.

In a more advanced class, the 'school' example in Chapter two, for example, the role play would have been impossible if certain facts about the two schools had not been known.

This information can be given to the students, or they can, as in the 'school' example, help to construct the facts themselves. The teacher should not underestimate the students' ability to judge their own needs with regard to such information, and should therefore allow this phase to be flexible.

One of the business people in a 'Bellcrest'[2] class of mine had become more and more frustrated about the lack of information on the firm's financial situation, so arrived one evening with five pages of financial details he had worked out himself. The role play planned for that evening had to be postponed until the rest of the class had a chance to consider the new material, but it helped to clarify a lot of questions, and the subsequent role play was much more realistic.

---

1   From B Abbs and I Freebairn *Building Strategies* (Longman 1978) page 118.
2   J Webb *The Bellcrest Story* (OUP 1973).

4.2.2 The class's pre-role play preparation

The class has been introduced to, and has practised, the material that the teacher has predicted will be necessary for the role play. The situation and the necessary facts surrounding it have been given out or discussed. The students now have their role cards and are ready to prepare their roles.

The amount of preparation time depends on the type and scope of the role play, and the type and scope of the individual role. Students merely going into a railway information office to ask the times of trains, etc. will only need a moment or two to jot down what they want to ask, while the 'railway official' will only need a moment to familiarise himself with the timetable. Students faced with a complex industrial problem to which a solution must be found, may need hours.

In the latter case, preparation may be done at home, but when this happens the teacher should make sure that the students with key roles will *be* at the next class meeting (and also, of course, that the preparation *will* be done!). It is usually an advantage, however, if the teacher is on hand to help with any problems which may arise.

If there are enough students to make more than one role play group, then students can prepare in twos or threes, thus helping each other. As preparation time will vary from student to student, and from group to group, it is obvious that students or groups will finish at different times. Role play groups can start as soon as all the participants are ready, or there can be small supplementary tasks available for those who have finished. For example, students who have to work out arguments for a particular point of view may be asked, if they have finished this, to see what arguments might be put forward for the *opposite* point of view, the better to counter them if they are raised.

4.3 The role play

4.3.1 Organisation

If there are two or more role play groups, then the available space should be organised so that they disturb each other, and are disturbed by external factors, as little as possible. Extra rooms, halls, corridors can all be used.

The teacher should make a plan of which students are in each group, and where each group should be, so that the practical organisation goes smoothly and quickly.

When deciding on the composition of the groups, the teacher should consider both the abilities and the personalities of the students. A role play group consisting solely of the shyest and quietest students will not be a success. Similarly, one 'weak' student should not be put into a group of 'good' students, or vice versa.

4.3.2 The role of the teacher

The teacher (see 3.3.1) may be taking a minor part in the role play. If not, then he should be as unobtrusive as possible. He is listening for general mistakes (i.e. mistakes made by several students) and particular mistakes (i.e. mistakes made by only one or two students, on more than one occasion). In the role play phase, the most important mistakes are those which hinder comprehension, and thus the smooth flow of oral interaction, for example: 'I have saw that film' is perfectly comprehensible, and would not cause even a native speaker to hesitate, but: 'Film, I yesterday, yes' requires some thought on the part of the listener, and therefore interrupts the conversational exchange.

No less important are mistakes in the acceptability and appropriateness of an utterance, especially when they show that the speaker has misunderstood the situation, the level of formality, the attitude of the other speakers, or the precise nature of his role.

Structural and lexical mistakes should not be *ignored* (e.g. 'I have saw' above), especially if they are being made by more than one student, but they are of less importance *in the role play* than the other mistakes mentioned above. They should, of course, be worked with at a later date.

As there are so many categories of mistake that can be made, it is a good idea to have a checklist, i.e. structure/formality, etc. so that short notes can be made under the relevant headings. Sometimes the teacher might choose to concentrate on one or two categories only, so as to have a clearer picture as to how well the students are coping under the chosen headings.

The teacher can make notes, or use a tape recorder. The advantage of the latter is that it can be replayed at leisure, no mistakes are missed, and the context in which the mistake is made can be referred to. To be fully effective, however, each group should have a tape recorder, and this is impossible for most classes. Also, if the tape recorders require the setting up of external microphones, the students may feel inhibited by their presence.

The best type of machine for the purpose is a small cassette machine with built-in microphone. One of these may also be used by the teacher, if the role play is of such a nature that he can walk round the groups with it in his hand. The quality of the resulting recording will not be of the best, but should be good enough to serve as the teacher's 'memory'. Only very motivated, specialised classes would wish for a good quality recording which can later be replayed in class for discussion and analysis.

The only legitimate time for the teacher to interrupt a role play is when it has broken down completely, i.e. the participants cannot get it to function. Here the task of the teacher is to stop the role play, and try to analyse, with the students, the reason for its collapse.

If, in spite of careful selection and preparation, it proved to be too difficult, then it should be left to a later lesson, and the students should go on to another activity.

It might be, however, that the group lacked some information or misunderstood the instructions in some way. In such cases the answer may be to stop the role play and discuss the missing information, or clarify the misunderstanding. The role play can then start again *from the beginning*. A role play which has been interrupted by the teacher cannot still be seen as role play, and must therefore have a new starting point. In the cases where the teacher does not have a role, there is a difference between teacher *interruption* and teacher *involvement*. One student in an advanced class, faced with a need for more information said, during a role play: 'I'm afraid I can't answer that, but I believe Miss Livingstone is in her office, she has been working on the problem – Miss Livingstone, would you come here a moment?'. Once I had given the information, I said I had 'another appointment' and left the group. This I judged a legitimate example of teacher *involvement*. Had the student wanted to consult me on a point of grammar, then he would have been consulting me in my role as teacher, and *interrupting* the role play.

4.3.3   Time
Adequate time should be given for each group to complete their role play to their satisfaction. As it is difficult to predict what is 'adequate', plenty of time should be set aside. Students who have to stop in the middle of a role play because the lesson is finished will feel frustrated, and feel that the time spent on preparation has been wasted.

When one or several groups finish before the others, they can be given a task related to the role play until the whole class is finished. This might be to make a report or summary of their findings, to answer a few questions about the exercise, etc.

4.4   Follow-up

As each role play is an integrated part of the total course plan, it will be followed up in subsequent lessons in a number of ways. The activities and exercises directly related to any particular role play will be discussed here.

4.4.1   Immediate follow-up
This does not mean the correction of mistakes, or even the pointing out of mistakes made. The role play is finished; if it has been successful, then the students feel satisfied and pleased that they have used the language for something concrete and useful. This feeling of satisfaction will quickly disappear if their every mistake is then going to be analysed and corrected. It may also make them less confident and fluent in subsequent role plays.

Immediate follow-up is a short phase where the whole class is together to find out what was done in the role play. At the most elementary level, a few questions can be asked (as in Chapter two, where two or three students were asked what they bought in the 'shops'). At more advanced levels, a report or summary of the groups' findings or decisions can be given. This phase need not deal only with fact: in a situation where a customer takes goods back to the shop to complain, the customer might be asked how friendly and helpful the shop assistant was, to see if the correct attitude was shown and understood.

This is a way of drawing the class together again, as a class, and making them ready for the next activity or exercise.

This phase can also take the form of an informal discussion about the formal composition of the role play. Did the students feel they had enough preparation? If not, what was lacking? Did their group work well? If so, why? If not, why not? Was there enough or too much information on their role cards or were there any other aspects they may wish to comment on? This should not be a follow-up to every role play, it would be very boring if it were, but it should be done formally a few times so that the students feel they are free to comment or criticise if they want to.

These criticisms and comments will help the teacher to improve the role play for future classes, and perhaps even give ideas for new role plays. The teacher may have prepared what *he* thinks is a good role play, but as he is rarely actually taking part in it, he cannot experience at first hand any drawbacks it may have.

4.4.2   Long-term follow-up
Long-term follow-up concerns the mistakes the teacher noted during the role play. Exercises designed to revise, practise, and so hopefully eradicate them, should form part of the ongoing activities of the class.

Subsequent role plays and other forms of freer work will show whether these exercises have achieved their aim, or whether yet more work will have to be done. Remedial exercises can be given either to the whole class, to groups of students making the same mistake, or to individuals.

From the teacher's point of view, the class's comments on, and criticisms of the role play, will help him to design more successful role plays, and role play preparation exercises.

Discussion

1   Discuss different ways of greeting people in your country (or the country your students come from). Compare them to the British (American, etc.) way. Note the differences in both language and behaviour.

2   Make a 'mistake' checklist as suggested in 4.3.1 above. Discuss what kind of mistakes would be acceptable within each category.

Exercises

1   Look at the example of a lesson based on buying clothes (see 4.1.1 above). Rewrite the role cards so that they now relate more closely to the lesson.

2   Using the same lesson as in question 1 and the section headings in this chapter, make notes under each heading for this lesson, so that you end up with a detailed plan of how you would lead up to, organise and execute the role play.

3   List a number of role play situations that would suit the needs, interests, and experience of *your* students.

Suggestions for further reading
1   On cultural differences see A Wright (1976) *Visual Materials for the Language Teacher* pp 3–4 and Chapter 7 Part 1. For pictures and text see D Morris (1977) *Manwatching*. For a more light-hearted view see G Mikes (1970) *How to be an Alien*.

2   On ways of expressing different functions see A Maley and A Duff (1978) *Drama Techniques in Language Learning* pp 19–26.

3   On predictability of language items see D A Wilkins (1972) *Linguistics in Language Teaching* pp 143–144.

5 Long-term preparation

The preparation described in detail in the two examples in Chapter two, and the points discussed in Chapter four describe the short-term preparation for a role play, i.e. the work immediately preceding, and relating to, a specific role play.

However, both Chapter three and Chapter four have indicated that such preparation, and the subsequent role play, can only be expected to be fully successful if the other oral activities done in class, the materials chosen as a basis for these, and the attitudes of the teacher and the class towards the learning situation are of such a nature as to make role play a natural and logical part of language learning.

This chapter discusses some ways in which this can be done.

5.1 Formal oral practice of language items

In this section the phrase 'oral practice' is taken to mean the formal, usually teacher-directed or teacher-led, exercises which are designed to practise a specific language point. Other forms of oral practice will be discussed in 5.2 to 5.5 below.

5.1.1 Traditional oral practice

The choice of the phrase 'oral practice' has been chosen deliberately as an alternative to the word 'drill'. 'Drills' are a form of oral structure/vocabulary practice which is closely associated with a behaviouristic approach to language teaching. Their main feature is a series of rigidly controlled stimuli and responses. Each exercise is designed so that each stimulus has only one correct response, for example:

Stimulus: I washed the car yesterday.
Response: I have just washed the car.
Stimulus: I saw Bob yesterday.
Response: I have just seen Bob. (*etc.*)

In the case of a stimulus that can be answered by 'yes' or 'no' there may be two correct responses, for example:

Stimulus: Do you like fish?
Response: Yes I do/No I don't.
Stimulus: Do you like pop music? (*coffee, this book, etc.*)
Response: Yes I do/No I don't.

This exercise, and a number of similar exercises, continues until the students are making automatic and structurally correct responses.

While it is obvious that the first example bears little or no resemblance to a real life oral exchange (and such drills are happily becoming rarer and rarer in the language learning classroom), it can be argued that the exchanges in the second example might well occur in real life. The second example has the added advantage that there is a choice of response, and the student can therefore answer truthfully.

But if the second exercise is examined more closely it will be seen that it is only marginally better than the first. There are several reasons for this:

(a) There is no theme or topic; fish and pop music have nothing in common. It is therefore difficult to develop or expand the exercise as it stands, or to practise the language in a communicative situation.

(b) There is a choice of response, but not a *real* choice; few people have such clear-cut likes and dislikes. The responses given are, in fact, rarely used alone as an answer to the question.

(c) It is not clear what the *function* of the question is. This relates to point (a) above. Only by very carefully examining each exchange can we be sure that the response is appropriate to the stimulus. Consider a similar exercise:

Stimulus: Have you got a dog?
Response: Yes I have/No I haven't.

Here the first speaker requires information, and the responses are acceptable, but unless the subsequent stimuli are chosen carefully, the following exchange might be produced.

Stimulus: Have you got a pencil?
Response: Yes, I have/No, I haven't.

A native speaker would assume this not to be a request for information, but an indication that the speaker wished to borrow the pencil, and respond: 'Yes, here you are/No, I'm afraid not'.

(d) There is no indication as to who the two speakers are, what relationship they have to each other, or in what situation they find themselves.

A communicative, meaningful oral exercise will take these points into consideration. This need not be as complex as it sounds; simple exercises, such as the 'Do you like?' example above can easily be improved. With this example in mind it can be assumed that:

(a) The situation is an informal social gathering.
(b) The two speakers have just met, so are therefore comparative strangers.
(c) They are therefore likely to be polite and friendly to each other.
(d) They would like to get to know each other better.

(e) They therefore have to find a neutral topic of mutual interests, and settle on music.

With this information it is possible to develop the example chosen: 'Do you like?' (see 5.1.3 and 5.1.4.)

5.1.2 Stimuli and responses

When two people are talking together they rarely have a third person at hand to cue their utterances. Therefore, although the teacher will usually present and initiate the exercise, it should be designed so that both stimuli and responses can be given by the students. In the example chosen this is easy enough (most students know the names of a number of musicians, pop groups and composers), but often there will be the need for some form of cue if the exercise is to run smoothly. This cue may be in the form of a simple cue card:

```
    Suggest going to _____ this evening.
```

Oral stimulus: How about going to the cinema this evening?
Oral stimulus: Let's go to the pub this evening. (*etc.*)

Pictures can also be used. (In this example the students making the responses have a map.)

Oral stimulus 1: Excuse me, where's the church?
Oral stimulus 2: Excuse me, where's the station? (*etc.*)

5.1.3 Choice
The exercise should contain an element of choice, so that the student can select, albeit from a limited range of responses, the response which is most appropriate to his own personal feelings. The example of a 'drill' in 5.1.1 above could, even at an elementary level, have a more realistic range of responses:

Stimulus:　Do you like _____?
Response:　Yes, I love _____.
　　　　　　Yes, I do.
　　　　　　Not really.
　　　　　　No, I don't.

Further choices can be added at a later point.

5.1.4　Extended exchanges
Given the information in 5.1.1 above, it can be seen that the stimuli and responses discussed so far are inadequate. Imagine a conversation based solely on the language used in 5.1.3:

A:　Do you like jazz?
B:　No, I don't.
A:　Do you like classical music?
B:　Yes, I do.
A:　Do you like Mozart?
B:　Not really.

Such a conversation is doomed to failure. A will soon regard B as uninterested and conversationally uncooperative.

'Yes I do/No, I don't' and similar yes/no answers are rarely used between mere acquaintances without further comment or clarification. Even at the elementary level such exercises can be made a little more natural by the use of a simple tag:

Example 1
A:　Do you like jazz?
B:　Not really, do you?
A:　Yes, I love jazz.

Students can also be encouraged to expand yes/no answers:

Example 2
A:　Do you like jazz?
B:　Not really. I like classical music.
A:　Do you like Beethoven?
B:　Yes, I love Beethoven.

These two exchanges are still not complete but they are more meaningful, acceptable and appropriate than previous examples. They can also be used as the start of a longer dialogue, of the type described in 5.2.2.3 below. Indeed, students should be encouraged to continue these exchanges whenever they are able to. An example of a complete, this time less open-ended exchange can be developed from the second example in 5.1.2:

A: Excuse me, where's the station?
B: In London Road.
A: Thank you.
B: Not at all.

5.1.5   Incorrect responses

Traditional structural drills are designed so that the possibility of making a structurally incorrect response is reduced to a minimum. With the type of exchange in 5.1.4 above this possibility is, however, very much increased. But a more open-ended exchange means that the student can try out his own hypotheses about the language, and have them confirmed or corrected immediately.

As already noted in Chapter three, a structurally correct answer does not always show the student's understanding of the language used. Incorrect responses, on the other hand, can indicate to the teacher how effective the teaching has been, how much the students have understood, and therefore how much more work will have to be done on that particular point. An incorrect response may also show that the student is *thinking* about the language, something traditional drills rarely require.

5.1.6   The information gap

'In classroom terms, an information gap exercise means that one student must be in a position to tell another something that the second student does not know.'[1]

This information gap is the essence of communication, we ask because we do not know, we tell because we want others to know. Two students are looking at a large clock and have the following oral exchange:

A: What's the time?
B: Two o'clock.

Here no information gap is present, no real communication has taken place. Such exchanges may be acceptable in the initial learning stages where the aim is to first illustrate meaning, then to practise pronunciation, stress, and intonation, but further practice of this type is meaningless. The example above becomes instantly more realistic if only B can see the clock: an information gap has been created.

Similarly, in the 'asking the way' example in 5.1.2 above, an information gap is created if both students have simple maps, but only the student giving

1   K Morrow in K Johnson and K Morrow *Communication in the Classroom* (Longman 1981) page 62.

the information has the church, station, etc. marked on his map. The second student will then have to listen carefully if he is to mark in the information he requires.

When dealing with more 'abstract' concepts such as personal opinions, the information gap is provided by giving a range of possible responses, and requiring an extended exchange to show that the first response has been understood.

5.1.7   Practical drawbacks

Oral practice of this type is more difficult to design than traditional drills. It is also more difficult to present and initiate. It takes more time, and the results are less predictable. It is, nevertheless, a more useful, natural and meaningful form of language practice.

5.2   Dialogue work

The first two activities in this section are a natural extension of the oral practice in 5.1 above. In class it will often be difficult to see any dividing line between the two. This is all to the good, as it shows that the work the students are doing has a logical progression, and forms part of a recognisable whole.

5.2.1   Skeleton dialogues

Skeleton dialogues give a very limited choice, and can be used where the situation and function are 'concrete', e.g. asking for and giving information at a station:

A: Excuse me, when's the next train to _____?
B: At _____.
A: How much is a _____ ticket?
B: _____.
A: And which platform does it leave from?
B: _____.
A: Thank you.

This dialogue can be put on the blackboard or overhead projector with the blanks filled in, and the complete dialogue practised (chorally or individually) to obtain acceptable pronunciation, stress and intonation. The class can then be divided into pairs, and one student in each pair given a simple railway timetable, for example:

Train to	*time*	*single*	*return*	*platform*
London	10.45	£10.00	£18.50	2
Cardiff	9.10	£15.00	£27.75	3
Bristol	11.20	£ 7.45	£13.60	5
York	12.35	£12.50	£24.00	7

The information can then be erased from the dialogue, so that it is left with blanks, as above. Each pair of students can then produce four dialogues, referring to the model if necessary.

Skeleton dialogues are easy to design when the dialogue deals with facts, as in the example above. When more abstract and personal concepts, such as giving opinions, expressing likes and dislikes, etc. are being dealt with, they are rather more difficult to construct.

5.2.2   Class composition of dialogues

This is a more difficult technique, at least from the teacher's point of view, than the skeleton dialogues above. It seems therefore relevant to give a more detailed description of it, in the form of a lesson sketch.

The function being practised is expressing likes and dislikes, at a beginners' level.

5.2.2.1   Presentation dialogue
The example in the textbook[1] is as follows:

Radio tonight

  7.00 Oscar Peterson – Jazz
  8.00 Berlin Philharmonic plays Beethoven
  9.30 Folk music from France

A: What's on the radio tonight?
B: Mmmm, do you like jazz?
A: Not really.
B: How about Beethoven?
A: I love Beethoven.
B: Good, so do I.

The model dialogue is presented and practised chorally and individually.

5.2.2.2   Formal oral practice
(a) As in 5.1.4 Examples 1 and 2.
(b) This requires a simple radio timetable similar to that in 5.2.2.1 above, which is given to only some of the students:

Stimulus: What's on at _____?
Response: _____.

---

1   C C Livingstone *Some Material for Beginners* (Studieskolen 1977) page 8.

These two practices can be integrated, and an extended exchange developed:

A: What's on at (*7.00*)?
B: (*Oscar Peterson*). Do you like (*him*)?
A: _____. (*etc.*)

Students can practise this in class and in pairs.

5.2.2.3 Class composition
A new radio timetable is given to some of the students. The teacher chooses the initial line of the dialogue and writes it on the blackboard:

A: What's on the radio tonight?

The students who have the timetable suggest a suitable second line. This is written down. The other students suggest a third line, and so on, until a complete dialogue is on the blackboard. At this level the first dialogue cannot be expected to be radically different from the textbook model, but subsequent blackboard dialogues (three or four would not be too many at this point) should be more adventurous. Each completed dialogue can be read in class or in pairs.

The task of the teacher during this phase is to tactfully reject incorrect or inappropriate suggestions, without going into depth as to why they are not suitable. Long explanations would only hinder the spontaneity of the exercise. Where several students are suggesting the same type of inappropriate or incorrect utterance, it may mean that some point has been misunderstood by the majority of the class. It will then be necessary to clarify the misunderstanding before proceeding with further dialogues.

5.2.3 Pair/group dialogues
After work of the type described in 5.2.2 above, the students can be asked, in pairs or threes, to compose their own dialogues. This will consolidate previous work, and show to what extent the material has been understood.

Experimentation should be encouraged, within the confines of the language already learned; translation from the mother tongue should be avoided.

The example below is from a beginners' class of multi-lingual adults, who had had about 14 hours formal teaching:

Dialogue by Hend and Nusiba
H: What's on TV tonight?
N: The news is on at 7.30. Would you like to see it?
H: Yes, I would, and you?
N: Yes, I would.
H: What's on at 8.00?
N: A jazz concert.

H: Do you like jazz?
N: Yes, I love jazz, do you?
H: Yes, I do.

'Would you like to see it?' shows a real feeling for the language. In previous lessons they had learned: 'Would you like a cup of tea?'. The transfer of 'Would you like?' is praiseworthy. They had trouble with the rest of the sentence, which was originally: 'Would you like look?'. I corrected it.

Instead of 'Yes, I would, and you?' they wanted to say: 'Yes, I do', but when asked to think about it suggested the correct version themselves.

It may be argued that this dialogue is not 'good' English, but it is the students' *own* language, and is really quite impressive if the amount of known language is taken into account. I have seen several much more unnatural dialogues in language teaching textbooks!

It is a good idea to collect these dialogues, and give each student a copy of them all for their notebooks. This gives the students the feeling that their efforts are being used for something, and demonstrates to them the variety and range of language the class has mastered.

5.3   Conversational techniques

5.3.1   Conversational 'fillers'

The dialogue written by Hend and Nusiba above does not look like natural conversational English. One of the reasons for this is, of course, the limited amount of English at the students' disposal. Another reason is the lack of what I will call conversational 'fillers'. These are the many words, phrases and sounds (e.g. 'oh', 'really', 'I see', 'mmm', 'you know', etc.) which often carry little or no meaning, but yet form part of what we recognise as natural-sounding conversation. If we wish our students' utterances to be as natural as possible, we must train them to use these correctly. The first stage is recognition. The students should be exposed to oral English where these words and phrases are used. This will be by listening to tapes, and by practising the model samples of conversational English printed in the textbook. (Note the use of 'Mmmm' and 'Good' in the dialogue in 5.2.2.1 above.)

The second stage is practice. A phrase or two might be included in the formal practices, for example:

A: What's on the radio tonight?
B: *Let me see* . . . Do you like jazz?

Freer practice can take place in the class composition of dialogues. In the example below, the class is composing dialogues about their activities on the previous day. The phrases: 'oh', 'really', 'I see', 'How _____ (interesting, nice, etc.)' are written at one side of the blackboard, and the students are asked to use them where possible:

A: What did you do last night?

B: I had a lovely dinner in town.
A: *How nice.* What did you have? (*etc.*)

Students can also be encouraged to use them when writing their own dialogues in groups or pairs.

A few of these 'fillers' can be introduced at the very lowest levels and a wider repertoire built up, an item or two at a time.

5.3.2 Avoidance techniques

All our students will, at one time or another, inside and outside the classroom, be faced with a situation where they cannot formulate an answer, or merely have nothing to say. In situations of this kind, silence is rarely acceptable, one is expected to say something.

In much the same way as described in 5.3.1 above, students should be trained how to move the conversation away from themselves, and on to somebody else, for example:

Well, I'm not sure, what do you think, A?
I'd like to hear what B has to say about that.
I agree with C, how about you?

Such phrases help to keep the conversation flowing smoothly, and make the student confident that he can cope with most situations. As few of our students will ever achieve anything like native speaker competence, training in the use of this technique is very important.

Another 'avoidance technique' is circumlocution. Even native speakers can momentarily forget even quite common words; our students may never have known them. Circumlocution is the technique of saying something in other words, or talking 'round' a word. For example: 'the time in the morning and the evening when everyone is going and coming from work, and there is a lot of traffic' when one cannot remember or maybe does not know the phrase 'rush hour'. Students should be encouraged to use this technique rather than asking for, or looking up, a translation from the mother tongue.

5.4 Group work

Classes which spend most of their language learning time under the direct guidance of the teacher cannot be expected to execute role play successfully. Classes used to working in groups and pairs on a variety of tasks will have little difficulty in adding role play to their repertoire of learning activities. Some types of group and pair work have been discussed in this, and previous chapters. The following points should serve as a quick checklist when preparing group work with the ultimate aim of role play in mind:

(a) Vary the types of group activities as much as possible.

(b) Make group tasks completely clear at the very beginning, so that work can proceed with the minimum of reference to the teacher.

(c) Vary the composition of the groups from time to time, i.e. do not always have the same students working together.

(d) Make sure the work is within the students' present linguistic competence. Prepare for it carefully.

5.5 Miming, games and drama

Younger children have few inhibitions about leaving their seats and miming or acting. Adolescents and adults often feel shy and embarrassed when asked to do the same things.

Unless these inhibitions can be broken down, the students will not be able to perform a role play successfully. Use of movement, gesture, facial expression, stress and intonation are all necessary if a role is to be fulfilled naturally and realistically.

Natural language is rarely produced in an unnatural situation, i.e. sitting immobile at a desk. A simple example of this is getting the students, in the first lesson, to introduce themselves to each other:

A: Hello, I'm John Brown.
B: Hello, I'm Mary Hamilton. Pleased to meet you.

Initial repetition of this exchange is done with the students at their desks. If the subsequent practice is done there, it will be difficult to get a really natural intonation. But if the students are asked to move around the classroom, smiling and extending their hands as they say the exchange, then the language will sound much more natural.

Miming, games and drama are three activities which help to prepare students for role play. As with role play itself, they should, in classes unused to them, be introduced slowly and carefully. A detailed examination of these three areas would be out of place here. Teachers who wish to examine them in more detail are referred to the reading list at the end of the chapter. A few ideas as to how they could be introduced to a class are given below.

5.5.1 Miming

This can be initiated with the students sitting at their desks. One student mimes an action, and the other students guess what it is:

S1: What am I doing?
S2: You're _____ing.
S1: That's right/No, I'm not.

Other questions could be: 'What did I do last night?', or 'What am I going to do tomorrow?'.

Several types of question can be asked if the action mimed has to do with a job:

S1: What's my job? (*miming*)
S2: Do you work outside?

S1: No, I don't.
S3: Do you work alone? (*etc.*)

In both of these exercises the teacher will mime the first example or two himself to show what is required. The teacher should exaggerate his actions, so that the students may feel less shy about their own actions.

5.5.2 Games

'What's my job?' above would also be included here. Other simple games which involve one or more students leaving their seats are:

(a) *Beginners' level: Where is it?* One student is asked to leave the room, while the rest of the class 'hides' a small object (a hat, book, etc.). The student is then asked to return to the room, and asks:

S1: Is it in a desk?
S2: No, it isn't. (*etc.*)

(b) *Intermediate/Advanced level: Alibis.* The teacher tells a little story of a burglary he claims to have seen on the previous day. He gives a description of two of the students, and says they were the people he saw taking part in the 'robbery'. The two students must then leave the classroom to decide on their 'alibi' (they were together at the time in question). While they are deciding on their story, the rest of the class considers what kind of questions they will ask them.

The 'accused' come back into the classroom, one at a time. The rest of the class notes down the answers the first 'robber' gives, then tries to get the second 'robber' to give the same details. If not, their 'alibi' is broken, and they are 'guilty'.

5.5.3 Drama

'Dramatising' dialogues should be a regular class activity. It is discussed in its simplest form in the example of the students introducing themselves in 5.5 above. In its most sophisticated form it may lead to the formal performance of a play in front of an audience.

The dialogues may come from a textbook, or be written by the students themselves (as in 5.2.3 above). Suitable pronunciation, stress and intonation should be discussed and practised, and action and gesture suitable to the situation noted. Wherever possible, simple props should be used, e.g. toy or real money, clothing (buying clothes in a shop, or just 'dressing up'), table settings and menus (restaurant or café), etc. These will also prove useful in subsequent role plays.

Groups can practise the 'performance' of their dialogue, and some groups might be asked to perform for the class.

5.6   Listening comprehension

The training of aural comprehension is a necessity in all language teaching which aims at communicative competence.

What the students will hear in the foreign language is usually far in excess of what they will say, and while our teaching can give oral command of a limited corpus of language which can be manipulated to cope with many different functions and situations, we can never predict or control what will be said to them. Wide classroom exposure to, and training in the comprehension of different types of spoken English, is therefore essential.

5.6.1   Implicit and explicit content

Most listening comprehension exercises are designed to check the comprehension of *what* is said, i.e. the face-value meaning of the words, phrases and sentences uttered. This is the explicit content. For example, the following interview[1] is on tape:

JENNY: I'm living in a *student hostel* in *London*.
                London's in the *south east of England*.
INTERVIEWER: How long have you been living in London?
JENNY: Well, for the past two years.
INTERVIEWER: And where have you lived while you've been here?
JENNY: In a hostel in Bayswater.

The questions the students have to answer after listening to this passage are:

What type of home does she live in? (*cottage, flat, etc.*)
Where is it? (*in a large town, in the country, etc.*)
Where is this located in Britain? (*south east, north west, etc.*)

Most taped material available for beginners and intermediate students is of this type.

Comprehension of explicit content is, of course, necessary. Equally necessary, if not even more important, is comprehension of *how* something is said, the implicit content. For example: 'How interesting' can be said in such a way as to mean:

(a) I am interested, please tell me more.
(b) I am bored, I do not want to hear any more about it.

Tapes should be available which make it possible to hear the answers to some, or all, of the following questions:

What is the relationship between the two speakers?
How do they feel?
How do they feel towards the topic or situation?
How do they feel towards each other?

1   B Abbs and I Freebairn *Building Strategies Teacher's Book* (Longman 1978) Unit 1 page 7.

What effect is speaker A hoping to have on the other speakers (and vice versa)?

What helped to give you the answer to these questions?

With this type of question the focus in on such features as formality, role, language function, and the use of stress, intonation, tone of voice, etc. to show attitude. Students must not only be able to recognise such features, and understand why, and in what circumstances they are used; they must also be able to use an ever-increasing number of them appropriately when formulating their own utterances.

5.6.2 Training recognition and use of implicit information

It has already been mentioned that most taped material available focuses on the recognition of explicit information. It is essential, however, that the recognition and use of the features discussed above with regard to implicit information should be trained as early as possible in the language learning programme.

Teachers will therefore have to listen carefully to the tapes which are available. Often there are some utterances which illustrate one or two of the required features. Exploitation of these will rarely be found in the teacher's notes, so, at the lower levels at least, the teacher himself will have to work out ways of doing this. Some simple examples are given below.

5.6.2.1 Listening for attitude

(a) The book this example is taken from[1] is designed primarily for intermediate students, but the exercise below could be used with a beginners' class. It is the only exercise of its kind on the tape, the rest of the taped materials being mainly for explicit listening.

Listen to these sentences on tape.
Are the men: a) interested   b) surprised   c) doubtful   d) bored?

JAMES:	I bought a new coat today.	
DAVID:	Really.	(a b c d)
PAULINE:	I saw Mary and Fred in town.	
MIKE:	Really.	(a b c d)
RITA:	I had coffee with my mother.	
PAUL:	Really.	(a b c d)
SALLY:	Shall we go to the theatre tonight?	
ALAN:	Maybe.	(a b c d)
LIZ:	Do you want to wash the car tomorrow?	
TONY:	Maybe.	(a b c d)

1   K Morrow and K Johnson *Communicate 1* (CUP 1979) page 9.

JILL: My mother says she likes your new coat.
EDDY: Oh.   (a b c d)

CHRISTINE: Bill phoned this afternoon about the football match.
FRANK: Oh.   (a b c d)

You can see that in English, the same words can express different feelings. It depends *how* we say them. You must learn *what* to say, and also *how* to say it.

Expressing your feelings, and understanding others who are expressing their feelings – these are also things you must learn to do in English.

The four attitudes can either be explained in the mother tongue, or even better, as they will be used often in subsequent exercises, explained by means of simple line drawings:

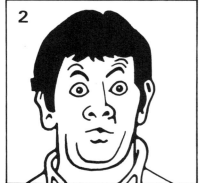

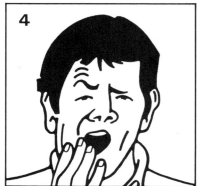

The exchanges are played one at a time, and after each one the students are asked how the second speaker feels. Where the students cannot agree, or are not sure, the exchange can be played again. They need say no more than 'face 1', 'face 2', etc. The tape can then be used as a model for repetition.

When the students can both recognise and produce the different attitudes, pairs could write similar exchanges and read them to the class. The class must guess what the attitude of the second speaker is.

An intermediate or advanced class might be asked what the next most likely utterance would be in each case, and then, in pairs or groups, build up a short dialogue. A pre-intermediate group of mine recently produced the following dialogue:

A: I bought a new coat today.
B: Really, what's it like?
A: It's mink.
B: Really? (*showing surprise*) Wasn't it expensive?
A: Yes, but it's my 50th birthday tomorrow.
B: Congratulations.
A: Thank you.

The voluntary use of the second 'really' shows that the group had gained a reasonable understanding of the use of the two different attitudes: 'really' (interested) and 'really' (surprised).

(b) This example is from material for intermediate students[1] and illustrates the point made earlier that a tape made for another purpose (in this case to illustrate the functions to be practised later in the lesson) can be used, if only for a couple of minutes, to train recognition of attitude. The questions which accompany the text are helpful in this respect.

BARBARA:	Rod? It's me, Barbara. Am I ringing at a bad time again?	
ROD:	No, no. That's all right. Is it something important?	
BARBARA:	No, not really. It's just . . . well, some American friends of mine are here for a few days and they wanted to go for a meal this evening. I thought maybe you'd like to come too.	5
ROD:	Well, that does sound fun, but . . . er . . . I'm afraid, I've got a bad headache, to tell you the truth, and . . .	
BARBARA:	Oh, have you? I *am* sorry. Why don't you take a couple of aspirins and lie down for a bit? You'll be all right in half an hour.	
ROD:	Yes, I know, but it's not just the headache. I'm afraid I really ought to do my washing this evening and I've got to write home to my parents too.	10
BARBARA:	Oh, well, shall we come round for a coffee later on instead?	
ROD:	Actually, I'd like to go to bed early tonight for once.	
BARBARA:	Oh, all right. Some other time then.	15
ROD:	Look, Barbara, I'll ring you at work some time tomorrow.	

1 B Abbs and I Freebairn *Building Strategies* (Longman 1978) page 57.

BARBARA: Don't you remember? I'm leaving for Italy tomorrow.
ROD: Oh, yes. Of course. So you are. I remember now.
BARBARA: Well, have a nice evening, Rod.
ROD: Wait a minute, Barbara. I'll ring you early tomorrow   20
         morning and . . .
BARBARA: It's OK, Rod. I understand – perfectly. See you around.
(*click*)

1   Is Rod alone in the flat when Barbara rings again?
2   Why does Barbara ring Rod? *She wants to invite him to* _____
3   Does Rod want to go? Why not? *No, because* _____
4   What excuse does Rod make first? *He says he's got* _____
5   What does Barbara suggest he does? *She suggests he* _____
6   What is Rod's next excuse? *He says he ought to*_____
7   What does Barbara now suggest? *She suggests that she and
    her friends* _____
8   What is Rod's final excuse? *He says he'd like to* _____
9   What do you think Barbara thinks? *She thinks Rod* _____
10 Do you think Rod wants to see Barbara again?

The teacher's notes[1] for this dialogue do little more than touch on the attitudes that can be heard on the tape. They suggest that, after the questions which check understanding of the explicit information have been answered, the teacher asks additional questions such as:

Do you think Rod was rude? Or stupid? Why?
Do you think Barbara believed Rod?

Some of the utterances can be investigated more closely than the above questions indicate:

ROD: No, no. That's all right (*said insincerely*) (line 2)

Questions
Does Rod mean what he says?
How would he say the same sentence if he did mean it?
(*Class repeats the sincere and insincere way of saying it.*)

ROD: . . . but . . . er . . . I'm afraid . . . (line 6)

Questions
Does Rod have a headache?
Why does he hesitate?
How would he say the sentence if he *did* have a headache?
(*Class repeats both ways.*)

BARBARA: Oh, all right. Some other time then. (*sounding disappointed, angry*) (line 15)

1 B Abbs and I Freebairn *Building Strategies Teacher's Book* (Longman 1978) page 60.

Questions
How does Barbara feel?
Do her words alone show these feelings?
What does? (*intonation, tone, etc.*)
If she didn't mind, how would she say this line?
(*Class repeats both ways.*)

Lines 17 and 19 can be treated in the same way as line 15 above.

BARBARA: See you around. (line 22)

Questions
Does Barbara expect to see Rod again?
What would she have said if she did?

The understanding the students gain from considering such questions will help to make the following repetition phase (also on tape) sound more realistic.

The oral exercises which follow this dialogue are designed to practise 'Inviting people to do things' and 'Refusing invitations politely and making excuses'. Once again, with the knowledge gained from the detailed investigation of the dialogue, the students are more likely to be careful when formulating their 'refusals' and 'excuses', so that they sound polite and sincere.

These two examples have shown how taped dialogues, not primarily designed for detailed investigation into para-linguistic features and choice of language, can nevertheless be so used.

Other taped materials useful for this purpose will be found in the reading list at the end of this chapter.

Exercises

1   Find one or two examples of traditional drills (as described in 5.1.1 above). What are they designed to practise? Design more meaningful oral practices for the same teaching points. How would you use these in class?

2   Look at a few illustratory dialogues from any language teaching textbook. How many conversational 'fillers' do they use? Choose a dialogue which is reasonably natural and realistic, but which has no 'fillers'. Rewrite it with 'fillers'.

3   How would you use the rewritten dialogue in question 2 above in class? How do your notes compare with any teaching suggestions given in the textbook (or accompanying teacher's book)?

4   How many types of group activity can you list? Would any of these be more suitable at any particular level? Give reasons for your answer.

5   Listen to any tape designed for listening comprehension. Comment on how natural it sounds (normal speed of speech, 'fillers', incomplete sen-

tences, etc.). Is it designed for listening for explicit or implicit content? If the former, could any part of it be put to the latter use? If so, what use and how?

Suggestions for further reading
1   On drills see D Byrne (1976) *Teaching Oral English* pp 36–43, J Dakin (1973) *The Language Laboratory and Language Learning* page 29 and Chapters 4 and 5 and W Rivers (1972) *Teaching Foreign-Language Skills* Chapter 4.

2   On information gap see K Johnson and K Morrow (eds.) (1981) *Communication in the Classroom* page 62.

3   On pair practice and dialogue work see D Byrne (1976) *Teaching Oral English* pp 59–76.

4   On cue cards see J Kerr in S Holden (ed.) (1978) *Visual Aids for Classroom Interaction* pp 42–47.

5   On conversational 'fillers' see G Brown (1977) *Listening to Spoken English* Chapter 6.

6   On group work see D Byrne (1976) *Teaching Oral English* pp 80–83, D Byrne and A Wright (1975) *What Do You Think? Teacher's Book 1* pp xvi–xvii.

7   On miming, drama and games see A Maley and A Duff (1978) *Drama Techniques in Language Learning*, S Holden (1981) *Drama in Language Teaching* and J Dixey and M Rinvolucri (1978) *Get Up and Do It!*

8   On games see A Wright et al. (1979) *Games for La.1guage Learning* and W R Lee (1965) *Language Teaching Games and Contests*.

9   On listening comprehension see G Brown (1977) *Listening to Spoken English* Chapters 1 and 8, D Byrne (1976) *Teaching Oral English* Chapter 3, D Crystal and D Davey (1975) *Advanced Conversational English* Introduction and Chapter 4 and A Wright (1976) *Visual Materials for the Language Teacher* Chapter 1.

Taped materials suitable for implicit listening
1   For beginners and intermediate students see V J Cook (1979) *Using Intonation* and A Maley and A Duff (1978) *Variations on a Theme*.

2   For advanced students see D Crystal and D Davey (1975) *Advanced Conversational English* and the dialogues in J Harmer and J W Arnold (1979) *Advanced Speaking Skills*.

6 Developing role plays

At the more advanced levels there are a number of excellent books (listed at the end of this chapter) which not only provide detailed role play situations and role cards, but also have a number of exercises which practise the language which will be needed in the role play.

Teachers of beginners and intermediate students are, as yet, less fortunate. Many materials for these levels give no guidance in how to use the material for role playing; others give merely a sketch of a role play, or role playing type activity.[1] It is therefore obvious that the teacher himself will have to initiate or develop his own role plays for these levels.

This chapter discusses ways in which this can be done.

6.1 Interviews

This is one of the simplest and easiest forms of role play to arrange. It can be used with almost any material based on oral English, and can easily be adapted to suit different topics, functions, etc. Briefly, one student pretends to be a certain person, and prepares a 'story'. The second student prepares questions to ask him, and then 'interviews' him.

Some stimulus (a picture, a piece of text or tape, etc.) is necessary as a starting point, and the type of interview should, of course, fit in with the aims of the rest of the lesson (or series of lessons).

Preparation cards can be written which focus on particular aspects of the stimulus, or may be designed so as to encourage students to use a particular language item (see 6.1.2). It should be emphasised that by this means the teacher *hopes* the students will use the items indicated; they should not be *required* to do so.

6.1.1 Interview – beginners

At this level, questions and answers will need to be reasonably 'concrete' (i.e. dealing with job, family, house, etc.). The stimulus should not, therefore, contain too much extra detail, or invite more 'abstract' language. If the person has an expression of, say, anger or sorrow, the students might want to ask questions like: 'Why are you looking so unhappy?'. Such questions, and suitable replies to them, are beyond the linguistic competence of beginners.

1 One set of materials for 'false beginners' which does give detailed role cards is M Knight and D Whitling *All Right* (Almquist and Wiksell 1978).

Even at this level, conversational 'fillers' and indirect ways of asking questions should be introduced, so that the interview does not resemble a police interrogation:

You live in London, don't you?
I see, and where do you live?
So you like your work? (*etc.*)

Replies should be short, i.e. not always full sentences, and show the interviewee's wish to cooperate:

Interviewer: You live in London, don't you?
Interviewee: Yes, in Battersea.

A full sentence answer here would sound unnatural:

Interviewee: Yes, I live in London.

While an unaccompanied 'yes' is also unnatural, people in this situation rarely answer with a simple 'yes' or 'no' more than a couple of times. Using the above picture as stimulus a class-composed dialogue (see 5.2.2 above) can be used to show how to deal with these types of questions and answers. A new picture is given out, and half the class prepares the questions, half the 'stories'. If role cards are necessary, they might look like this:

Role 1

You are the person in the picture. Say your name. Tell about where you live, about your job, about your family (married? children?). Tell about what you do in the evenings and at weekends.

> **Role 2**
>
> You are interviewing the person in the picture. Ask
> his name. Ask what his job is, and where he lives. Ask
> when he starts work, etc. Ask about his family
> (married? children?). Ask what he does in the
> evenings and at weekends.

Preparation can be done in pairs, and the students can make short notes if
they wish. The students then re-form into pairs of interviewer and interviewee, and the interview takes place.

6.1.2 Interview – intermediate

As the girl in this picture has a definite expression on her face, the students
may be encouraged to ask the more 'abstract' kind of questions which were
discouraged in the previous example. The role cards have been designed to

encourage the use of the present simple: 'Every day I . . .' and the use of 'like/hate/enjoy' with the gerund: 'I enjoy dancing'. Further indirect questioning techniques should be practised in the preparation phases:

That sounds interesting, could you tell me more about it?
You don't seem to like your job? (*with question intonation*)

With classes used to this type of activity, the class composition phase should not be necessary at this level.

The role cards might look like this:

Role 1

You are interviewing the girl in the picture. Ask her about herself (name, age, family, etc.). Ask her about her job (hours, duties, what she likes/enjoys/hates about it). Ask her about her spare time and what she likes/hates/enjoys about her life in general. Remember not to ask too many direct questions.

Role 2

You are the girl in the picture. Give details about yourself (name, age, family, etc.). Tell about your work (hours, duties, what you like/hate/enjoy about it). Tell about your spare time and what you like/hate/enjoy about your life in general.

Interviews need not be limited to personal questions: the stimulus might deal with an event (an accident, a demonstration, etc.). In this case the interviewer asks about the person's experience of the event. The number of roles need not be confined to two: a married couple could be interviewed (perhaps about how inflation and rising prices have affected their family) or two people who were standing together and saw the same event could be interviewed together. It is perhaps requiring too much of any one 'interviewer' to interview more than two, or at the most, three, people together.

6.2 Development of a role play on one theme

Previous chapters have stressed the importance of continuous, carefully planned development of the student's knowledge and active command of all aspects of linguistic competence and role behaviour. One way in which this can be done is by expanding role plays based on one situation. Each successive role play revises the language (in its broadest sense) required in the previous ones, while adding another dimension to the situation.

The example given here is asking for information at a travel office.

6.2.1 Beginners' example

Role 1

You work at the station. Help the customer.

The next train to York
    leaves at 12.15
    from platform 6
    arrives in York at 15.15
    single ticket £18.00
    return ticket £32.00

Role 2

You want to go to York. Ask about the next train, the platform. Ask about the price of a _____ ticket, and buy one.

Similar role cards can be written for other destinations.

6.2.2 Intermediate example

This deals with more than one form of transport, and requires the 'customer' to compare travelling times and prices. The basic functions, asking for and giving information are the same.

Role 1

You work at the travel agent's. Help the customer.

EDINBURGH	*journey time*	*single*	*return*	*departures*
Train	5 hours	£27	£50	7.20, 8.45, 10.00, 11.30, 12.55
Plane	55 minutes	£50	£96	7.00, 9.00, 11.00, 13.00
Bus	8 hours	£19	£40	8.00

Role 2

You want to go to Edinburgh in the morning. Ask about
prices and times (you want to go reasonably quickly and
cheaply). Find a suitable way to go and buy a ticket.

6.2.3   Advanced example

This example would come after discussion of different types of holiday, and
was developed by Marielise Berg-Sonne to accompany Unit 6 of *Kernel Lessons Plus*[1]. The figures are adapted from *Project Great Britain – Holidays and Festivals*.[2]

The emphasis here has shifted from means of travel to accommodation,
but the basic functions have not changed. Comparison has been expanded
to include not only prices, but also facilities. Other functions and language
needed will be obvious from the role cards.

On the opposite page you will find the information sheet which is given to
the travel agent. This should be referred to when working through the role
play. (Role 1 is given below, and Role 2 on page 74.)

Role 1

You work at a travel agent's in London. Look at the
information sheet. Discuss the meaning of any words
you don't know with the people you work with. Then
discuss which language you will need to:

Greet your customer and find out what you can help
him/her with. Explain what possibilities there are
regarding types of accommodation and activities.
Recommend what's most suitable, and suggest
alternatives. (Remember you are there to *sell*.)

If he/she books a holiday remember to get the name
and address.

1   R O'Neill *Kernel Lessons Plus* (Longman 1972)
2   Patience Thom *Project Great Britain – Holidays and Festivals* (Mary Glasgow
Publications 1977)

South Coast Holidays

ACCOMMODATION

Camping   Many good sites, but crowded in July and August.
Book in advance at Tourist Information Centres.

Cottages   Self catering. Prices: £40–£200 per week. Book
early through travel agent.

Hotels   FAMILY HOTELS – especially good for families with
younger children.
Prices: £4.00–£8.00 B & B. Evening meals extra.
SMALLER HOTELS – mostly on the coast. Small, max. 20
bedrooms, few extra facilities.
Single rooms: £7.00–£16.00
Double rooms: £9.50–£27.00

LARGER HOTELS

Name	Price per person B & B and evening meal	Facilities
Holiday Inn	£10 a night £50 a week	TV in all rooms, garage, bar, etc.
Continental	£14 a night £70 a week	Private baths in all rooms, swimming pool, TV, bars, etc.
Duke of Cornwall	£18 a night £80 a week	TV, private baths, tennis courts, swimming pool, etc.

ACTIVITIES

Riding   Including tuition – from £33 per week.
Fishing   Excellent. Permit about £20 per week.
Shooting   £10.00 per gun per day in season.
Golf   Several courses. Special visitor's permit £10.00 per week.
Boat hire   Oct.–May from £75 a week.
June–Sept. from £125 a week.

Role 2

You are Mr and Mrs _____. You are going to go on
holiday for a week to the south coast. Choose a name.
Decide how big your family is, and if you are going to
bring the children. You can afford to spend £175
(remember pocket money and travelling expenses).
Discuss how you can ask the travel agent about:

accommodation (camping, cottage, hotel, etc.)
facilities (TV, swimming pool, etc.)
meals (included in price)
activities you may be interested in (golf, fishing,
riding, etc.)

Go to the travel agent's and get the information you
need. Discuss which possibilities will suit you best. If
you decide to book a holiday, do so. If not, make a
good excuse.

Even though the class is not using *Kernel Lessons Plus*, this role play can
still be built up, using hotel and travel brochures (available in English from
most big travel agents). Students can then see the kind of place they are
booking holidays for. The texts of such brochures can provide reading practice (looking for information, assessing the style of advertisements, etc.).

The follow-up of this role play might take the form of letter-writing. The
'customers' could write a letter to a friend, telling him about the arrangements they have made for their holiday. The 'travel agents' could write letters booking the accommodation, etc.

6.3 Using existing materials

It was noted in the introduction to this chapter that few beginners' and intermediate materials give sufficiently detailed role play situations, or role
cards. Many of the newer 'functionally based' materials, and those that aim
at 'communicative competence' take many of the aspects of role behaviour
into consideration, and provide excellent presentation and practice phases
for them. When this preparation is already part of the material, developing
detailed role plays is relatively easy.

6.3.1 Beginners' examples
These two examples come from *Follow Me*.[1] In this material the terms that
indicate a possible role play situation are: Improvisation, Transfer, Role
Playing, About you.[2]

1 L G Alexander and R H Kingsbury *Follow Me 1* (Longman 1980).
2 L G Alexander and R H Kingsbury *Follow Me Teacher's Book 1* (Longman 1980)
page 7 point 4: Improvisation.

Example 1[1]

Context Practice/Improvisation
S1 an English-speaking visitor to this town stops S2 and S3, two residents, in the street. Begin like this:

S1: Excuse me.
S2: Yes?
S1: Is there a restaurant near here?
S3: Yes. There's one /in Market Street/.
    It's very good. I like it very much.
S1: Thank you very much.
S2: There's one /in South Street/, too.
    I prefer that one.
    It's /the Market Restaurant/.

Continue to cover spelling; address (and precise location); telephone number; likes/dislikes ('Do you like /Italian/ food?'); regular opening times; the time now; restaurant open/closed now; leave-taking and thanks.

This is clearly not a role play as defined in this book. The main drawback is the lack of information. If a stranger asks you something in the street, you either have the information he requires or not, you do not make it up as you go along. Apart from being unrealistic, this only makes the already complex task of oral communication even more complex. For a role play based on this situation to be realistic and for it to run smoothly, the students must have ready access to the relevant information.

The teacher's notes[2] for this exercise are very general, and indicate a guided dialogue composition (see 5.2.2 and 5.2.3 above) rather than a role play. This guided dialogue work may be done as part of the preparation.

Role play cards similar to those below can then be given out:

Role 1

You are a stranger in town. You want to eat dinner. Stop someone and ask about restaurants. Ask where they are, what kind of food they serve, when they are open, etc. (You like Italian food.) Remember to thank the person(s) and say goodbye.

---

1   L G Alexander and R H Kingsbury *Follow Me 1* (Longman 1980) Unit 8 page 31.
2   L G Alexander and R H Kingsbury *Follow Me Teacher's Book 1* (Longman 1980) pp 17, 18 and 68–69.

Role 2

Help the tourist. Here is some information:

Restaurants

The Pork Pie (English food)
Market Street
Open 11.00–2.00 and 6.00–9.30
Good food, quite cheap.

La Porta (Italian food)
Birch Street
Open 6.00–11.30
Good and cheap. (This is your favourite.)

Carlton Grill (French food)
Town Hall Square
Open 11.00–3.00 and 6.30–10.30
Very good, very expensive.

Role 3 contains the same information as above, but with a different 'favourite restaurant'.

The students are given a few moments to study their role cards, and then do the role play.

Example 2[1]

Improvisation
S1 arrives at a hotel abroad and asks to see a foreign friend who is staying there. The receptionist, S2, asks for S1's name and the name of the friend. The friend is not in /his/ room, but S2 asks for a description in case /she/ has seen /him/ in the hotel and knows where /he/ is.

Once again, there is not enough information provided to make a realistic and smooth-running role play. It can be dealt with as in 6.3.1.1 above, with the following role cards:

Role 1

You go into the Ascot Hotel, where your friend Bob Evans is staying. Ask the receptionist which room he has, and if he is in his room. Describe Bob to the receptionist.

1   L G Alexander and R H Kingsbury *Follow Me 1* (Longman 1980) Unit 12 page 48.

(The student is given a coloured picture of a person from a magazine.)

> **Role 2**
>
> You are the receptionist at the Ascot Hotel. Mr Evans
> has Room 357. He is not in his room. Ask for a
> description of him. You saw him go _____ a
> moment ago.

Various different names, room numbers and pictures can be used.

6.3.2 Intermediate examples
Another common form of 'role play' in current textbooks is where two roles
are written out side by side in almost diagrammatic form[1]:

You wake up one morning and (as usual in England) the sun is shining, the
birds are singing, and there's not a cloud in the sky! You decide to go to the
seaside for the day. So you phone a friend . . . Your partner is the friend.
Practise like this:

You

Invite your friend.
Say why you want to go.

The friend

Accept the invitation.
Suggest how to go.

Accept your friend's suggestion.
Make arrangements when and
where to meet.
Finish the conversation.

Make arrangements when and
where to meet.
Finish the conversation.

Another example[2] may be seen in the diagram on page 78.

It is not surprising that these exercises are so similar. At the lower levels the
students have only a limited amount of language at their command, so that
books which teach the same functions will often come up with the same
practice situations. What is missing here is the information gap. Both students are using the same diagram, so each will know what the other is going
to say. (The teacher's notes for the first example[3] do suggest that each student looks only at his 'part' and covers the other with a piece of paper, but
many students read ahead in the book before class; others will be inclined

---

1   From K Johnson and K Morrow *Approaches* (CUP 1979) page 32.
2   B Abbs and I Freebairn *Building Strategies* (Longman 1978) page 23.
3   K Johnson and K Morrow *Approaches Teacher's Book* (CUP 1979) pp 31–32.

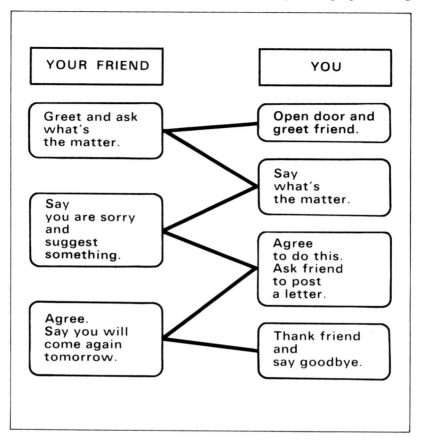

to 'cheat' by moving the paper.) Also, the way the diagrams are built up often makes them difficult to follow. A third drawback is that having to refer to a book limits the naturalness of the exercise. It is much easier to have all the information on one small card, so you can move around and make gestures without losing your place.

As with the beginners' examples, this type of exercise is more suited to guided dialogue work. Role cards are easy to manage, and make the exercise more realistic:

Role 1

It is a lovely hot summer day. Your friend phones you.
You would like to go out today, but you do not want
to go to the beach. Say what you would like to do.
Agree on something to do, and arrange when and
where you will meet. Say goodbye.

Role 2

It is a lovely hot summer day. Phone your friend. Find
something you would both like to do (you make a
suggestion first). Agree on a time and place to meet.
Say goodbye.

More practice is given if there are different sets of role cards, so that pairs
can do more than one role play, for example: 'It is a lovely hot summer day'
can be changed to 'It is a cold winter evening', 'It is a rainy Saturday morning', etc. 'You do not want to go to the beach' will be changed accordingly:
'You do not want to go to the cinema', 'You would like to go to a museum',
etc. The cards above are 'neutral' as regards age, i.e. they are equally suitable for children or adults, but they could be designed to suit a particular
age group:

Role 1

It is Tuesday after school. You phone your friend.
Find something you would both like to do tonight.
Agree on a time and place to meet. Say goodbye.

Role 2

It is Tuesday after school. Your friend phones you.
You would like to meet him/her this evening, but have
some homework to do first. Find something you would
both like to do. Agree on a time and place to meet.
Say goodbye.

After a little practice, the teacher will find that the writing of these cards will go quickly and smoothly, and if the cards are written on stiff cardboard for example, and kept carefully (I put each set of cards in a plastic folder which can be inserted into a ring file), then they will last for a very long time.

Exercises

1   'Interviews need not be limited to personal questions: the stimulus might deal with an event' (see 6.1.2 above). Find a picture, piece of text or tape which shows or describes an event (an accident, a demonstration, etc.). Design role cards for an interview situation with the people involved in the event (write cards for both interviewers and interviewees). Say at what level you would use this role play, and give a short sketch of how you would prepare for it.

2   Write some more sets of role cards for one of the intermediate examples in 6.3.2 above.

3   The examples in 6.3.2 are at an intermediate level. Design a role play with the same basic function of 'Inviting' for a more advanced class (you might, for example, include levels of formality and making excuses). Write sample role cards.

Suggestions for materials and for further reading
1   Multi-skills courses which contain detailed role plays and role cards. For false beginners see M Knight and D Whitling (1978) *All Right*. For advanced students see J Harmer and J W Arnold (1979) *Advanced Speaking Skills,* D Hicks, M Poté, A Esnol and D Wright (1979) *A Case for English SB/TB* (role cards in Teacher's Book) and J Webb (1973) *The Bellcrest Story* (business English).

2   Books or sets of cards for role plays. For intermediate students see P Watcyn-Jones (1978) *Act English SB/TB* and S Porter (1980) *Action Pack.* For advanced students see F Heyworth (1978) *The Language of Discussion* (includes preparatory exercises), M Lynch (1977) *It's Your Choice,* S Menné (1975 and 1977) *Q-Cards,* S Porter (1980) *Action Pack,* G Ramsey (1978) *Play Your Part* (includes preparatory exercises) and P Watcyn-Jones (1978) *Act English SB/TB.*

Appendix: some simple role plays

For those teachers working with materials which do not include role plays or ideas for role plays, this appendix gives some examples which might provide starting points for a class's role play activities.

Classes or teachers who have never tried role playing before are advised to start with an example that is well within the students' linguistic competence, i.e. an intermediate class might start with a beginners' example, and an advanced class with an intermediate example. Beginners' classes could start with the first example below, or with the simple interview in 6.1.1 above.

Beginners

1

> **Role 1**
>
> You meet _____ in the street. You are fine. Ask
> _____ if he/she would like a cup of tea/coffee in a
> café. There is a nice café in _____ Street.

> **Role 2**
>
> You meet _____ in the street. Ask how he/she is
> (you are fine). You would like a cup of coffee.

2

> **Role 1**
>
> You meet _____ in the street. You are fine. You
> ask _____ to have a drink with you. Go into the
> pub, ask _____ what he/she would like to drink,
> and get it from the bar.

Role 2

You meet _____ in the street. You are not well
(headache). You would like to sit down. You would
like a double whisky and an aspirin.

Role 3

You are the barman in the pub. Beer costs 60p a pint.
Whisky, gin, etc. cost 65p. Soft drinks cost 25p. Wine
costs 55p a glass.

3

Role 1

You go to a restaurant with _____. Ask about a
table. Ask _____ what he/she wants. Ask if he/she
wants a bottle of wine with the meal. Order the food
and drink. Pay the bill.

Role 2

You go to a restaurant with _____. Look at the
menu and tell _____ what you would like to eat and
drink.

Role 3

You are the waiter. You have a table for two. Give the
customers a menu. Take their order. Give them the bill.

The waiter will, of course, have a menu provided by the teacher, or written
by the class. Role plays 2 and 3 can be adapted for children by making the
situation a coffee bar and a hamburger bar respectively.

4

Role 1

You go into a hotel and ask about a room. You want a
_____ room for _____ nights. Ask about the
price (with/without bathroom). Sign the hotel register.

Role 2

You are the hotel receptionist. Help the customer.
You can give him the kind of room he wants.

one night	with bath	without bath
single room	£20	£18
double room	£30	£27

Ask him to sign the register.

5

Role 1

You are in a new town, at the railway station. You
want to go to the Palace Hotel. Stop someone and
ask the way.

Role 2

You are at the railway station. Help the tourist.

(The student playing Role 2 has a map.)

Intermediate

It can be seen that many of these role plays are developments of the beginners' examples.

1

Role 1

You want to have a party at the weekend. Discuss with your friends where to have it (your parents have guests all weekend), who to invite, what to eat and drink and who will buy it, and which records you want.

Role 2

You want to have a party at the weekend (but not Friday, as you are going out). Discuss the details with your friends. You are free on Saturday morning, so can help with the preparations.

Role 3

You want to have a party at the weekend. Discuss the details with your friends. You do not want to lend your records, as two were damaged the last time.

Role 4

You want to have a party at the weekend. Discuss the details with your friends. Your parents let you use the cellar, as long as there is nothing stronger than beer to drink.

The number of roles here is very flexible, but four is probably an ideal number, as it gives plenty of room for some discussion, but not so much that agreement becomes difficult. This can be adapted for adults, in which case the alcohol and record problems could be exchanged for problems of who one should or should not invite.

A suitable follow-up to this example might be phoning up and inviting the people the group has agreed upon, or writing them a short note.

2

Advertisement

Small, second floor flat in Queen Street to rent. Suit student. £75 a month. Phone Mrs Evans, 457683.

Role 1

You see an advertisement in a newspaper. Phone up and find out more about the flat. Make a note of the things you want to ask about before you phone. If the flat sounds suitable, arrange to go round and see it.

Role 2

You have a flat to rent. You put an advertisement in the newspaper. Someone phones up about the flat. Answer their questions. (Think first about what they might ask, and have the answers ready.) If the person is interested, arrange for him/her to come and look at it.

Weaker students might need some cues as to what questions they might ask or be asked, for example:

Role 1

Ask about the number of rooms, about central heating, about furniture, etc.

Role 2

Be prepared to answer how many rooms there are, if there is central heating, if it is fully furnished, etc.

3

Role 1

You are on holiday in England. You bought an expensive dictionary (for your English classes!) two days ago. You have discovered that 20 pages are blank (show them to the assistant). You have lost the receipt. You want your money back.

Role 2

You work in a bookshop. Ask the customer if you can help him/her. Ask if he/she is sure the book was bought in your shop. Ask for the receipt. Offer to order a new dictionary (you have no copies left).

This can be developed to cover all kinds of faulty goods (shoes with broken heels, faults in clothes, etc.).

4

Role 1

You lost a _____ on the train/bus to _____ yesterday at _____ (time). Go to the lost property office. Describe what you lost (colour, size, material, etc.). None of the _____s the attendant shows you are yours. Ask him/her what you should do now.

Role 2

You are the attendant at a lost property office. Ask the person what he/she has lost, and where/when it was lost. Ask him/her to describe the object in detail. Show him/her some objects. Suggest he/she comes back tomorrow.

5

> **Role 1**
>
> You work at the Savoy Hotel. Help the customer. You have no double rooms with bath vacant for tonight.
>
> | one night | with bath | without bath |
> |---|---|---|
> | single room | £40 | £35 |
> | double room | £50 | £45 |
>
> restaurant – ground floor, top floor
> bar – ground floor, 3rd floor
> nightclub – top floor
> swimming pool – 3rd floor
> hairdresser – 2nd floor
> car park – basement

> **Role 2**
>
> You are at the Savoy Hotel. Ask about the prices of rooms and book one for tonight. You are hungry, thirsty, and would like a swim.

Perhaps more relevant would be information about smaller, family hotels, guest houses, and bed and breakfast accommodation for which cards can also be designed along these lines, but everyone likes a little luxury too!

Advanced

1

> **Role 1**
>
> You work in the overseas department of Bolton Brothers. You are on a business trip. You are in your hotel lounge, writing reports. You are tired, and want peace and quiet. You do not want to talk to anyone. You do not want to go out tonight, but finally agree to. Be polite, but negative.

Role 2

You are in your hotel lounge. You want to watch TV.
If you can't do that, then you might as well chat to
someone. You think you recognise the other person in
the room. You have recently visited the firm of
Bolton Brothers. It might be there that you met. Try
and strike up a conversation, and invite the other
person out tonight. Try to persuade him/her.

This, on the surface, seems a simple situation, but Role 1 involves knowledge of, and ability to produce, attitude. Role 2 requires the rather difficult function of persuasion.

2

Role 1

You are the waiter at the Rooftop Restaurant. Help
the customers. The roast lamb is excellent. There is no
salmon left.

Role 2

You are taking two friends out to dinner. Ask them
what they would like to eat and drink, and order from
the waiter.

Role 3

A friend is taking you out to dinner. Say what you
would like. You love fish.

Role 4

A friend is taking you out to dinner. Say what you
would like. You are a vegetarian.

Here we have a restaurant situation again, this time with a few problems built in. A menu is, of course, provided with roast lamb and salmon marked on it.

3

This role play was developed by Ian Cocker as part of a series of lessons on the problems of underdeveloped countries. The students are given the following background information:

Child's name: Blavadino Mansilla
Sex: Male
Age: Seven
Born: Jolo, an island in the Philippines
Language: Visayan
Living conditions: Most people on the island are fishermen, smallholders, day labourers or vendors of foodstuffs and other small merchandise. Jobs are scarce, many are unemployed.

Families live in makeshift or semi-permanent houses made of bamboo or nipa palm with salvaged galvanised iron roofing. These houses are built on stilts over water, and crowded together in villages. Sanitary conditions are poor, medical facilities almost non-existent, and disease consequently very common.

Diet consists mainly of rice, with a little fish and vegetable when available. Clothing minimal.

Blavadino is one of five children. His parents have always tried their best for them, but there is never much money. His father suffers from arthritis, and is unlikely ever to work again. The parents have the choice of trying to have one or more of their children adopted, or seeing them go hungry.

> **Roles 1 and 2**
>
> You are Blavadino's parents. You have decided to have your son adopted. Describe how you came to this decision. Describe your family, how you live, and why you want your son adopted.

Further roles for this role play – those of social workers and prospective adoptive parents – are given on the next page.

Roles 3 and 4

You are social workers. You must decide what is to happen to Blavadino. Interview his parents (age/school/living conditions, etc.). Interview the Danish couple who want to adopt Blavadino. Find out about their background, and what they can offer the child. Find out *why* they want to adopt him, and if they are aware what the problems may be. Remember this is a difficult situation for all concerned, so your questions will need to be less direct and more tactful than usual.

Roles 5 and 6

You are the Danish couple who want to adopt Blavadino. You must be prepared to answer detailed questions about yourselves and your way of life. Have you thought of the problems involved in adopting a Philippine child?

4

This role play was developed as part of a series of lessons on 'traffic problems'.

After initial work on the picture[1] (discussion of the problem, how the various characters are feeling, etc.), the class is divided into two groups (or four, if a large class; six or seven would not be too many to have in one group). Each group should come up with a solution to the problem:

Either (a) A solution which would please environmentalists, and the local committee for the preservation of old buildings.

or (b) A solution which would please the more commercially-minded elements in the town.

The solutions may be in the form of a diagram, or notes, or both. Where there are more than two solutions, the best of each type should be chosen. All the students have a chance to study the solutions.

A meeting of those interested is called, and the solutions discussed. Obviously, roles can be added or subtracted as necessary.

Role 1

You are a member of the council's traffic committee. You must lead the meeting, and make sure everyone gets their say. You yourself must remain neutral.

Role 2

You are John Oxton (the man waving the stick in the picture). You own one of the old houses in the town centre, as did your father before you. You hate noise, traffic, oil companies and the 'laissez-faire' attitude of the council.

Role 3

You are Henry Adams, manager of an oil company. There is a route avoiding the town, but it puts another 60 kilometres on the journey. Time costs money. You think wanting to preserve old houses is pure romanticism, they are falling down anyway, and probably insanitary.

---

1 Picture 7 'Juggernaut' (opposite) from D Byrne *Wall Pictures for Language Practice* (Longman 1976). Several suggestions for the exploitation of this picture can be found in the *Teacher's Book* pages 90–105.

Role 4

You have recently bought the pub in the town square.
More traffic means more custom, and you know that
the council is bound to find you new, and probably
better premises if they pull down the existing buildings
to widen the road.

Role 5

You are the young mother in the picture, and leader
of the committee for the preservation of old buildings.
You want your children to grow up in a clean,
traffic-free environment.

An extra written task, either before or after this role play, might be the
writing of letters to the local paper, putting forward the various points of
view.

Bibliography

Abbs, B and Freebairn, I *Building Strategies SB/TB* (Longman 1978)

Alexander, L G and Kingsbury, R H *Follow Me 1/TB 1* (Longman 1980)

Allen, J P B and Corder, S P *The Edinburgh Course in Applied Linguistics Volume 3* (OUP 1974)

Brown, G *Listening to Spoken English* (Longman 1977)

Brumfit, C J *Problems and Principles in Language Teaching* (Pergamon Press 1980)

Byrne, D *Teaching Oral English* (Longman 1976)

Bryne, D *Wall Pictures for Language Practice SB/TB* (Longman 1976)

Byrne, D and Wright, A *What Do You Think? Teacher's Book 1* (Longman 1975)

Cook, V J *Using Intonation* (Longman 1979)

Coulthard, M *An Introduction to Discourse Analysis* (Longman 1977)

Crystal, D and Davey, D *Advanced Conversational English* (Longman 1975)

Dakin, J *The Language Laboratory and Language Learning* (Longman 1973)

Dixey, J and Rinvolucri, M *Get Up and Do It! SB/TB* (Longman 1978)

Harmer, J and Arnold, J W *Advanced Speaking Skills* (Longman 1979)

Herbert, D and Sturtridge, G *ELT Guide 2: Simulations* (NFER/The British Council 1979)

Heyworth, F *The Language of Discussion* (Hodder & Stoughton 1978)

Hicks, D, Poté, M, Esnol, A and Wright, D *A Case for English SB/TB* (CUP 1979)

Holden, S *Drama in Language Teaching* (Longman 1981)

Holden, S (ed.) *Visual Aids for Classroom Interaction* (Modern English Publications 1978)

Johnson, K and Morrow, K *Approaches SB/TB* (CUP 1979)

Johnson, K and Morrow, K (eds.) *Communication in the Classroom* (Longman 1981)

Jones, K *Nine Graded Simulations for Communication Skills* (ILEA 1974)

Knight, M and Whitling. D *All Right* (Almquist & Wiksell 1978)

Lee, W R *Language Teaching Games and Contests* (OUP 1965)

Leech, G and Svartvik, J *A Communicative Grammar of English* (Longman 1975)

Livingstone, C C *Some Material for Beginners* (Studieskolen 1977)

Lynch, M *It's Your Choice* (Edward Arnold 1977)

Maley, A and Duff, A *Drama Techniques in Language Learning* (CUP 1978(b))

Maley, A and Duff, A *Variations on a Theme* (CUP 1978(a))

Menné, S *Q-Cards* (Paul Norbury Publications 1975 and 1977)

Mikes, G *How to be an Alien* (Penguin 1970)

Morris, D *Manwatching* (Jonathan Cape 1977)

Morrow, K and Johnson, K *Communicate 1* (CUP 1979)

O'Neill, R *Kernel Lessons Plus* (Longman 1972)

Porter, S *Action Pack* (Edward Arnold 1980)

Ramsey, G *Play Your Part* (Longman 1978)

Revel, J *Teaching Techniques for Communicative English* (Macmillan 1979)

Rivers, W *Teaching Foreign-Language Skills* (University of Chicago Press 1972)

Rivers, W and Temperley, M S *A Practical Guide to the Teaching of English* (OUP 1978)

Rogers, J *Adults Learning* (Open University Press 1977)

Thom, P *Project Great Britain – Holidays and Festivals* (Mary Glasgow Publications 1977)

Watcyn-Jones, P *Act English SB/TB* (Penguin 1978)

Webb, J *The Bellcrest Story* (OUP 1973)

Wilkins, D A *Linguistics in Language Teaching* (Edward Arnold 1972)

Wilkins, D A *Notional Syllabuses* (OUP 1976)

Wilkins, D A *Second-language Learning and Teaching* (Edward Arnold 1974)

Wright, A *Visual Materials for the Language Teacher* (Longman 1976)

Wright, A et al. *Games for Language Learning* (CUP 1979)